HELP ME SPEAK

HUMAN HORIZONS SERIES

HELP ME SPEAK

*A Parent's Guide to Speech
and
Language Therapy*

JENNY BARRETT
M.A., M.C.S.L.T., Cert.Ed.

*A Condor Book
Souvenir Press (E&A) Ltd*

First published 1994 by Souvenir Press
(Educational & Academic) Ltd,
43 Great Russell Street, London WC1B 3PA
and simultaneously in Canada

ISBN 0 285 63180 2

Photoset by Rowland Phototypesetting Ltd,
Bury St Edmunds, Suffolk

Printed in Great Britain by
The Guernsey Press Co. Ltd, Guernsey, Channel Islands

For my beloved parents

Contents

Introduction 9
1 The Local Clinic: The First Line Of Help 15
2 Language And Its Problems 39
3 Specialist Help Pre-School 62
4 Language Disorder 90
5 Learning Difficulties 115
6 Physical Disability 135
7 Autism 159
8 Other Factors Affecting Speech and Language 179
9 Integration 203
10 The Charities 222
Glossary 233
Assessments 236
Sound System 242
Useful Addresses 243
Bibliography 246
Index 251

Introduction

Language, and the ability to speak fluently, are vital to all of us. Without speech we are deprived of one of the most important ways of communicating; without speech we become isolated, divorced from the world around us. Some would say that speech is our single most vital attribute. To be able to communicate our thoughts, feelings and aspirations in this way makes us a unique species. When this skill fails to develop, or is impaired by accident or injury, the result is great anguish, despair and frustration. Communication breakdown is no respecter of persons. Anyone, at any time in his or her life, can be bereft of speech. Ten million people is a staggering statistic which should concern all of us, but it is for the many millions of parents whose children are included in that statistic that this book has been written.

Communication impairment is devastating at any time in life, but for children it is particularly damaging, for it disrupts every aspect of their lives—their learning, their self-esteem, their relationships with others. It never ceases to amaze me how uninformed most people are about these children and their problems.

Unlike other disabilities there is nothing to show, no damaged arm or leg, to engender sympathy and understanding. It truly is the hidden handicap.

So it is to speech and language therapists that parents turn for advice, guidance and therapy. Yet, despite all our exceptional skills, there are still far too few people who have the vaguest idea of what we do. Perhaps even more alarmingly, there are some people who do not even know that we exist. For many, other than those allied professionals with whom we work, such as health workers, educational psychologists and teachers, we are an enigma.

Many people suspect that we are in some way related to the acting profession and see us as middle-aged spinsters with posh accents, dressed in matching twin set and pearls, concocting our professional brews somewhere in Hampstead, Cheltenham or a remote region of the Shires. Never for a moment would men be considered part of our fraternity. Although far too few in numbers, our male colleagues bring their own special brand of excellence to the profession.

Speech and language therapy is a relatively new profession, only some eighty or so years old, but in that time every part of the community has benefited in some way from our skills, including actors, parliamentarians and broadcasters. There was even a monarch, and at least one prime minister, who received speech therapy.

Thankfully the Cheltenham stereotype is a myth. Speech and language therapists are highly trained professionals: during their years of study they will have delved into psychology, linguistics, anatomy, neurology, physiology, phonetics and a whole host of other related '-ologies', as well as clinical management and the rudiments of how to operate a personal computer. Walk into any speech therapy clinic, and the engaging young lady dressed in nondescript blouse and jeans, seated on the floor surrounded by children no doubt spellbound by the antics of the puppet she has on her hand, will more than likely have an honours degree. Her colleague, working with another group, may well have a Master's degree as well as a teaching qualification. Between them their achievements represent more than ten years of study; in addition, they will have accumulated several hundred hours of in-service training, honing their skills to meet the demands of our complex society.

Since its early years the profession has flourished. In Britain there are well over 4,500 speech and language therapists: some are practising in the remote regions of the Outer Hebrides, others in the deprived areas of our inner cities, while others have patients in prisons, schools, hospitals of various kinds and the plush holiday resorts of the South Coast. Quite literally, the lame, the halt and the blind have found their way to their neighbourhood speech and language clinic. Even babes in arms, only days old, have been helped by a therapist.

Since I entered the profession some thirty or more years ago, the way in which we approach our work within the community has changed dramatically. In the intervening years therapists have achieved for themselves wider recognition; at the same time we have placed upon ourselves even higher professional standards. It is rare these days for young therapists to work in isolation, as I did.

How well I recall, within weeks of graduation, taking on the air of a modern Florence Nightingale as I sallied forth, eager to dispense my skills in a school in London's East End.

Other professionals have always found the East End to be a rewarding experience; equally, I was not to be disappointed. On arrival I was told that under no circumstances should I roam through the school alone; as in some penal institution, I was to be escorted at all times by a male member of staff. Obviously female members of staff were vulnerable to student molestation of one kind or another. Staff room chatter was far more enlightening: one female staff member had certainly been raped, while others were continually harassed by various forms of body touching and bottom pinching. It was after a group of pupils tried to set fire to the kitchen, with staff imprisoned inside, that I decided it was time to depart!

All that was a long time ago. In the intervening years speech therapy has led me to diverse places: from Harlow New Town to the foothills of the Canadian Rockies where my patients included Indians from the Blackfoot Nation and children from the local Mennonite population, an austere religious farming community. Canada taught me to be resilient and resourceful. Clinics might be remote church halls, family homes or schoolrooms. Our 'parish' covered several hundred square miles and winter mornings nearly always began with clearing the snow and ice from around our mobile team transit van.

Today's young therapists are far better equipped to deal with the problems awaiting them in society. The majority of degree courses are now four years compared to my own three, and include such diverse subjects as computer skills and managing a clinic. Newly qualified therapists are no longer presented with a caseload and told to 'get on with it'. Their early years are continually nurtured and monitored by senior therapists, who guide them through complex cases and advise on the increasing amount of administration.

It is a wonderful and satisfying profession. Our rewards are certainly not monetary ones, but the compensations are there—like the small hand-drawn card I received from one of my young clients. With delightful simplicity it said: 'Mrs Barrett, thank you for helping me to speak.'

Over the years parents have asked the same kinds of questions, and it is in response to these recurring themes that I have structured this book; it is not intended to be a treatise for my colleagues. Everything I have written will be known to any one of them. You will notice that I have referred to all speech and language therapists as 'she' and all the children as 'he'; this is not intended to be chauvinist, it is for the sake of expediency, so that my readers are not distracted to the point of boredom by political correctness. I have also used 'therapist' and 'speech therapist' to describe our profession, which recently changed its name to 'speech and language therapists'. Again this is to avoid being pedantic, and for the same reason I have referred to children's communication difficulties by a variety of terms that mean the same thing.

The children discussed in the book do not represent any living individuals; they are compilations of children I have worked with over the years, with one or two exceptions whose parents have given their permission to quote their children's case histories.

I should like to take the opportunity to thank everyone who has helped me through the writing of this book—my colleagues, friends and my faithful black moggie who shared most of the early mornings and late nights beside the word processor. Special thanks go to Belinda, without whose secretarial skills I would have been lost, to Scott Muir, for his painstaking work on the graphics, and to my beloved husband John, without whose experience and support this manuscript might never have been completed.

Finally, thank you to all the children with whom I have worked over the years, for it is from them that I have learned the most.

Lewes, East Sussex
1993

1   The Local Clinic: The First Line Of Help

In our well-informed, communication-sated society, it is surprising that some parents still do not appear to know how or where to find a speech and language therapist. Even though there are still too few of us and the demand for our skills is continuously increasing, we are not an altogether elusive breed. Once found, therapists are friendly, sympathetic and, above all, excellent listeners.

On a quiet Friday afternoon, not so long ago, whilst clearing away a mountain of paperwork before the weekend break, I was interrupted by a gentle knock on the door. An anxious mum, accompanied by her small son, entered and exclaimed, 'Thank goodness I found you. I'm so worried about David's speech, finding you has been a nightmare.' Thankfully, this situation is rare, as these days the public are far better informed of the services that the National Health Service can offer.

As with many things in life, it is a matter of knowing where to start, then finding your way around the bureaucratic maze. The first signpost is the one telling you where to find your local speech and language therapist. We really are just round the corner. You need look no further than your local health centre or health clinic, where a wide range of services is provided by the local Health Authority. These may be found in a local general practitioner's (GP) practice or located in a separate building, hence the two different terms. As most health centres are situated in a town centre, you should have no difficulty locating yours. More than likely, there will be a large noticeboard informing the visitor where various departments and personnel can be found and when they are likely to be there.

So, as well as the speech and language therapist, who are all these other professionals in the 'health team', whose names you see neatly placed on the doors up and down the corridors? The list will read something like this: health visitors, district nurses, clinical psychologist, dentist, audiologist, clinical medical officer and, maybe, a visiting psychiatrist.

THE REFERRAL

What do you do once you have located your local therapist? It is not at all complicated, although I know from experience how unaware parents can be about the actual process of requesting a speech and language assessment, commonly known as a referral. What they may not appreciate is that speech and language therapists operate an 'open' referral system, which means we will take referrals from anyone, parents as well as professionals. All that is required is a phone call giving us a brief description of the problem, together with your child's date of birth, address, and the name of your doctor. There is no need to consult any other professional like the doctor or the health visitor. On the other hand, some parents prefer to consult their friendly health visitor before approaching the speech therapist.

Health visitors are really marvellous people and a mine of information, since it is their job to monitor babies' development from the day they are born. Understandably, parents sometimes feel very unsure whether their concerns are purely imaginary or whether there really is something wrong with their child's speech and language. The best advice, always, is to discuss your concerns with your health visitor and, should there be any problems with your child's speech, she will either make a referral or informally discuss the difficulty with the speech therapist.

These informal chats are very enlightening. Andrew had

not been seen by the health visitor for some time, and in the intervening period appeared to have developed a speech problem. From her point of view his speech, she said, sounded rather nasal in quality and she was puzzled because as far as she could tell everything inside his mouth was working properly. Andrew was seen by the therapist as soon as possible and, sure enough, his speech was very nasal, reminiscent of a child with a cleft palate. At this point Andrew did not need therapy, but was referred to an ear nose and throat (ENT) consultant for an assessment. Within a few weeks he reported that he had discovered a rare condition known as a submucous cleft, a hidden cleft of the palate in which the bone has not completely joined and yet is covered over by the mucous membrane lining of the mouth. A few months later Andrew had a successful operation to repair the cleft, and the nasality disappeared from his speech. Undoubtedly, it was the keen observation of the health visitor alerting the therapist to a potential problem, which saved Andrew from the destructive handicap of incoherent speech.

Our open referral policy means we have children referred to us from a whole range of professional colleagues as well as health visitors. However, because of their surveillance programme which covers the pre-school years, health visitors refer most of the children in this age group and also, since they are attached to GP practices, we tend to get fewer referrals from the GPs themselves. Clinical medical officers who work in the community and visit schools send us children, as do consultants, psychologists and teachers. Figure 1 shows the most common referral routes at the local clinic.

The Right Age for Referral
Therapists are frequently asked what is the best time to refer a child for therapy, and invariably the answer is, 'As soon as you notice a problem.' In an ideal world we always prefer to see a child sooner rather than later. Speech and language therapy departments may have different guidelines regarding the minimum age of referral for children at the

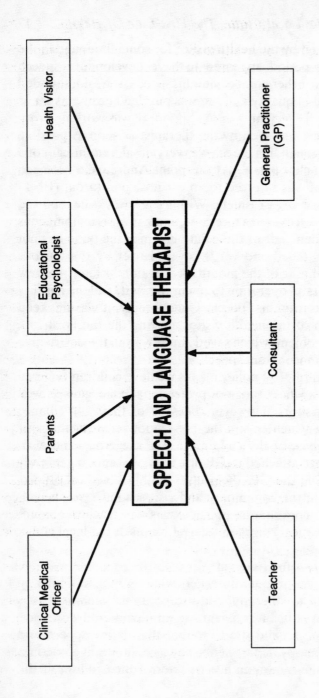

Figure 1. Common referral routes to the speech and language therapist at the local clinic.

local clinic, but generally there is a consensus that problems will become apparent any time between two and two-and-a-half years. One day, no doubt, when our knowledge of the early signs of language problems has improved through research, it will be possible to begin intervention much earlier in a child's life. After all, if we acknowledge that communication begins at birth, how much more productive it would be to start providing help at that time, rather than later.

If there is such a thing as a typical child, it would be Craig who was referred at the age of two-and-a-half. He had been slow in both understanding and developing language to use, and at two years he was using gesture and making a few vowel-like speech sounds. Craig was a first child, and with no brother or sister against whom to measure progress, his mum, although a little worried, consoled herself that he wasn't doing too badly—until she took him to the local mothers and toddlers group, where she discovered to her amazement and concern that other children of Craig's age were word-linking and having 'conversations'. She wondered if Craig was having hearing difficulties, even though he had been checked at nine months when all was well. In a state of high anxiety she contacted her health visitor who, equally concerned, referred Craig for a speech and language assessment. After he was assessed, Craig's mum was given some ideas on how to promote his understanding of language. When he was three years old he joined a pre-school language group of children with similar difficulties. Over the next two years he made excellent progress, and by the age of five it was possible to discharge him.

Sometimes parents are given advice from various sources which, as therapists, we would view with a certain degree of suspicion. How often have we heard the phrase 'he will grow out of it', which is a dangerous assumption and should set the alarm bells ringing. Remember that only speech and language therapists have the training, knowledge and expertise to tell you whether or not your child has a problem.

In recent years we have become increasingly aware of the link between early language difficulties and the problems children later experience in learning to read and spell. What is more, we cannot ignore the effect poor communication has on esteem, the making of friendships and becoming socially acceptable. Frustration and anger in small children can be difficult to handle, but in older children it can boil over into unacceptable anti-social behaviour. What began as a communication problem has now become a behaviour problem. Parents who are unaware of our open referral policy have the right to insist on a referral to the speech and language therapist if they have any concerns about their child's development of speech, language, fluency and voice—in fact any area of human communication. It is most unwise of other professionals to dismiss parental concerns and tell them to return if their child does not improve.

Without doubt, the very worst situation for therapists is to have referred, at five years of age or older, a child who has dreadful speech and language problems. David is one such example: he was eventually referred at the advanced age of thirteen years; a bright, intelligent boy, he had somehow managed to go through his school career without anyone suspecting the true nature of his learning difficulties. David had been educated for much of his life in private schools. Apparently, early failure in the local school had convinced his parents he needed a smaller class and far more support for his reading and spelling difficulties. This certainly helped for a while. However, David's behaviour began to deteriorate as again he failed to make progress with his schoolwork.

When he was twelve years of age he was eventually sent to a school which specialised in teaching secondary age children with reading and spelling problems. It was whilst he was there that an astute teacher noticed how David did not always understand what was said to him, or what was being discussed around him, and his frequently inappropriate replies to apparently simple questions. As soon as possible a referral was made to a local speech therapist for an assessment. David was subsequently found to have a serious language disorder.

How was it David managed to get so far without anyone noticing the problem? In retrospect it is easy to see how, with his intelligence and natural charm, he had developed this marvellous ability to cover up his problem, and it was only when he could no longer cope in school that his behaviour deteriorated. Mistakenly, his teachers thought it was his poor reading and bad behaviour that were causing him to fail, both of which had deflected attention away from the real cause, his language difficulties.

Parents, it must be said, may be the culprits: either unwilling to acknowledge that a problem exists, or hoping against hope that the problem will disappear. From experience I know that parents frequently feel guilty; many feel they have done something wrong, or have failed to do the right thing at the right time. It really is immaterial. No therapist will be critical, for we are there to provide sympathetic and professional guidance, and even if parents have made mistakes, we can give advice on how best to overcome the problem. It is most unlikely that a child's difficulty is caused solely by parents doing the wrong thing. No doubt the speech problem would have happened, no matter what you had or had not done.

After Referral
So what happens after the referral has been made? In most therapy departments, the following is the usual procedure. Within a week or so you will receive an acknowledgement of the referral, indicating that your child is now on the waiting list to be seen for an assessment. It will be accompanied by an information sheet, informing you of the name and location of the clinic where your child will be seen, how long you might need to wait, and frequently what to expect on your first visit. In order to save time, some departments send out a short questionnaire for parents, asking them

about their child's general development and his communication difficulty, to return completed, prior to the first appointment.

Sometimes parents contact us about the length of time they have to wait before assessment, since waiting lists, much in evidence in the media nowadays, are always a cause of concern for everyone working in the National Health Service. It is important to understand that all speech and language therapy departments have agreed to follow up referrals within the minimum time. Irrespective of understaffing, speech therapists have made a determined effort to reduce waiting times. Serious understaffing can push waiting times to three, four, even five months, no matter how imaginative the programme to deal with the problem, although this is an exception. Usually, you will wait no longer than two months, and frequently four weeks or less.

There are good reasons for trying to keep waiting times for initial appointments to a minimum. You will recall how therapists receive the majority of their referrals from other professionals, or 'agencies' as they are sometimes called, which means that until we actually see the children we have no idea of the severity of their problems. This information helps us plan our time more effectively, since we have a better idea of the needs of the children.

We constantly remind ourselves of the distress caused to children and parents by a prolonged wait for help. One mother eloquently summed up the anguish of having to wait six months for a first appointment (no one, I hasten to add, waits that long in my department!):

It was my own sense of guilt and isolation which threatened to overwhelm me. My child desperately needed help and so did I. All I could do was watch him grow older.

First Appointment—the Initial Assessment
The day arrives to see the speech and language therapist. As I mentioned in my Introduction, parents frequently have very little idea what we do and how we do it. Many mistakenly believe we only help children say their sounds and cannot understand why, when a child can say his sounds, he has been referred to us for an assessment. Although public perception of our work has improved, many people still believe we are elocution teachers by another name. Some years ago, I well recall one rather large, aggressive lady marching into my room, pointing an accusing finger at me and shouting, 'So you're the lady what's gonna make my Davy talk proper.' There was little I could do but agree!

It is important to make parents feel at ease, so we begin by explaining what we intend to do during the session. An assessment is not a test for you and your child, reminiscent of the old 11+ examination, but a means of discovering what the problem is, what the cause might be, and then deciding what should be done.

Approaches to Assessment
At the local clinic there are different ways of dealing with assessment: jointly with several therapists working as a team, or a therapist seeing a child individually.

Joint assessment
With this approach, two or three therapists arrange to see a maximum number of children, usually no more than eight at any one time. Each agrees to undertake specific tasks. For example, one might interview parents, whilst the others between them observe how the children play and respond to some of our special tests. Sometimes it is possible to see more children by working this way, whilst at the same time having the benefit of a colleague's experience for those children with severe and complex speech and language difficulties.

One-to-one assessment
Your child may well be seen by one therapist who will carry
out procedures very similar to those described for joint
assessments, or we may undertake a 'screening', which is a
rapid assessment procedure taking about half-an-hour. We
use this more frequently when there are long waiting lists,
in order to find out the kinds of problems the children are
experiencing. Those with severe and complex difficulties will
require a further, more detailed assessment, which we can
then arrange at a later date. In a large and very busy clinic
this can be most effective as a 'rolling programme'—which
means that screening is repeated every four months, or
sometimes six months, for a period of a week by several
therapists. It is a most effective way of keeping waiting lists
under control, being efficient with our time. No one
approach is necessarily better than another, just different.
Most busy speech and language therapy departments will
use all these approaches to assessment throughout the year,
depending on their caseloads.

Parents also have preferences. Some prefer the more intimate contact offered by one therapist, since they feel less
exposed and vulnerable than if included in a group. Others,
however, enjoy the security and companionship of parents
with similar problems. There is a certain sharing of the
burden, when parents can meet others whose children have
speech and language difficulties similar to their own. Nothing can be more demoralising for parents than the feeling
of isolation they experience as a result of their child's poor
speech.

ASSESSMENT

Assessments are a joint undertaking by therapists and
parents. Parents will be asked a lot of questions about their
child's development; the therapist will be observing him at
play, with yourself, with brothers, sisters and other children,

noting his attention, listening and co-ordination, and in some cases will use some special tests. Naturally, with older children—those who are more than five years old—we would be less interested in play, and would be doing more complex assessments.

Figure 2 shows you the main parts of the whole assessment procedure. My best advice is to be prepared for the stream of questions we need to ask and to share information about your child. Some mothers understandably find it very difficult to recall all the information required and I think it is a good idea to bring along the baby book that many parents keep, charting their child's development. A 'case history' is just what it says: a complete history from the time of pregnancy to what your child is like today. It will cover the following:

— Speech and language development in as much detail as you can recall, with dates if possible. It is helpful to know what happened and when it happened.

— Your child's reaction to his speech and language problem. Is there any frustration, bad behaviour, or tantrums? If so, how do you handle it?

— Family history. Has anyone in the family had a speech/language problem? If so, who and what type of problem was it?

— Family details. Brothers and sisters; how many and ages. Parents' occupations. How do the brothers and sisters deal with the problem? Do they speak for him, ignore him, tease him, bully him?

— Other milestones:
   crawling
   sitting
   (at what age and in what order did these occur?)
   walking
   clean/dry

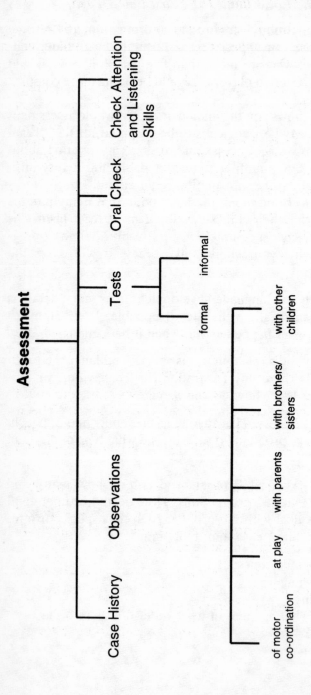

Figure 2. Main parts of the whole assessment procedure at the local clinic.

— Health history. Any serious accidents, illnesses, operations, ear infections? Details of when, and of any hospitalisation.

— Pregnancy and birth. Were there any difficulties in pregnancy, such as high blood pressure or bleeding? Was the birth straightforward? If not, what happened—for example, Caesarian section, forceps, breech birth? What was birth weight? Were there problems following birth, such as breathing or feeding difficulties? Did the baby have any problems sucking or swallowing?

— How does your child mix with other children? Does he or she play with them, have friends (depends on age)?

— Educational progress (if of school age). Any problems with skills associated with spoken language, such as reading and writing? Any special problems noticed by teacher?

— Other behaviour. How does your child relate generally to the world? Have you noticed any obsessions, rituals, tantrums, specific likes or dislikes?

— Hearing. Is there a history of any problems (this could have been covered under health history) and has it been checked recently? In many districts a referral to therapy is accompanied by an automatic referral for a hearing check.

— Vision. Has it been checked, any problems noticed?

— Co-ordination. Does your child fall over, drop things? Is he unable to catch/kick a ball/hold a pencil correctly to draw or write (depending on age)?

— Feeding. Does your child have any problems with sucking, chewing or swallowing, and have you noticed an unusual amount of dribbling?

— Attention and listening. Are these appropriate for his age?

Such a barrage of questions may appear rather formidable, and even with careful explanation some parents are not always clear why therapists require such detailed information. I recall one mother who objected rather noisily, demanding to know what on earth her pregnancy had to do with her child's speech problem—not an unreasonable protest. However, it is important for parents to realise that all the questions asked are extremely relevant, since they enable us to build up a complete picture of a child, not just a current snapshot. Therapists are searching for possible causes of a child's speech and language problem and it may be there in any one, or several, of the answers.

All of us like to have a pleasant area in which to work, and speech and language therapists are no different. Working areas vary considerably even within one district, depending on the age of the building in which the room is located and just how much money has been spent to make it as comfortable as possible. We all know what we would like as an ideal workplace, whether the room is located in a custom-built centre, or in an older building which has had to be adapted. Large and busy clinics occasionally have several rooms set aside for therapists, with the luxury of a separate office.

Parents are often pleasantly surprised when they put their heads round our door for the first time. Perhaps the medical connection of our work has evoked the picture of something resembling a doctor's surgery, but nothing could be further from reality. Most people think they have entered the local nursery or a small version of Toy World. You will find plenty of soft toys of all sizes, and some, like our elephant, are larger than most of the children we see. We have the farmyard, the dolls' house, the shop, puzzles, puppets and a whole range of constructional toys—and no self-respecting therapist would be without a post box, and that delight of all children, a teddy.

Play is a natural medium of communication, and by the way they play we can learn a great deal about children's language. If you think about it, toys are representations of the real things in the world, what therapists refer to as 'symbols'. For example, a dolls' house and all it contains represent a real house and its contents; toy people represent real people, and toy objects real objects. Any adult who enters into the make-believe world of children's pretend play knows how much the children understand about the toys or symbols and their relationships to each other. Therapists are interested to know whether or not the children have learned the verbal symbols—that is, the words for all of these symbols. By now you will have begun to appreciate why part of the assessment will be to observe how your child plays. Of course, we are aware of what is usual for a child at any particular age, since play, just like other aspects of a child's behaviour, has a developmental sequence. So what type of play might alert us to a problem?

Michael's play was by no means typical of a three-and-a-half year-old child. A chubby little boy with red hair, he entered the room without acknowledging the therapist. Not a look or a smile. Most children at this age are rather shy at first, clinging to their mother's hand in grim determination, but the very least they will do is look at you. Michael, however, as if drawn by a magnet, went directly to the box of miniature cars, carefully took them out and proceeded to line them up in one long, neat, straight row, all facing the same way. He then put them carefully back in the box, and then continued to repeat the whole performance, over and over again. At no point did he utter a sound, none of the usual childlike 'brrumm, brrumm' sounds, or accompanying squeals of delight. His play appeared to be completely lacking in any imagination or pretence.

Being an only child raised on a farm, with parents who both worked from dawn until dusk, Michael had lived in isolation; his lack of personal contact with other children, as well as adults, had not only been instrumental in bringing about problems of understanding language, but also he had not yet learned how to respond appropriately to others, even when language was not required. Within months of being introduced into the stimulating environment of a nursery, with the support of the speech therapist, his language had improved dramatically, although he remained a rather odd little boy who did not seek out the company of other people. When he was five he was discharged from therapy.

We can learn a great deal by watching the way in which children with language difficulties behave towards their parents, brothers and sisters and other children. I well recall Mark, who was the most accomplished manipulator of other human beings I have ever encountered. His delightful mother was desperately anxious about Mark's lack of speech, since he appeared to understand everything that was said, at least as well as the average three-year-old. However, he only ever grunted when he wanted anything—not a very happy state of affairs. He was accompanied to the clinic by a very caring older sister, who treated Mark as if he were her baby.

Mark proceeded within minutes to demonstrate his admirable skills in getting exactly what he wanted, when he wanted it, without uttering a word. If there was no response to his demand, he would immediately have a tantrum which prompted either his mother or his sister into action. Once the family became aware of what they were doing, life changed for Mark and within a few months he was beginning to use language, the tantrums ceased and his overall behaviour improved.

Tests of every description have become part of people's daily lives. As part of our assessment procedure we use them to check children's understanding and use of language, and of course parents are always curious to know more about the testing process. Some of these tests give us an 'age level', which means we are able to chart the actual age at which a child is either understanding or using language—for example, Johnny, at the age of five years, might be understanding language in the same way as a two-year-old.

Other assessments give us a 'profile' of a child's language. Usually a sample of language is collected from talking about pictures or playing with a child, and then the recorded sample is transcribed and analysed. We can find out from this, for example, the range and type of vocabulary, the grammatical constructions, and the type of questions being used; also it will enable the therapist to see whether the language produced was appropriate to the original questions asked. Quite rightly, there is nothing particularly wrong with the response 'I'm five', unless it is in answer to the question 'How are you?'

One such profile entails showing a child a series of pictures and asking questions to which there are predictable replies. It is very useful, because instead of transcribing hours of tape-recording, the therapist can target a particular aspect of grammar and see whether the child can use it in his speech. It is a quick and efficient way of getting a language sample.

John, who had recently started school, was suspected of having some difficulties with his language development, although the teacher wasn't quite sure exactly what these might be. When seen by the therapist, he was given this particular assessment. He was shown a picture depicting a mother and a boy in the bathroom; the question asked was, 'Mummy wants to know whether the boy has cleaned his teeth, so what does she say?' The usual response might be something like, 'Have you cleaned your teeth?' or variations on this depending on the child's use of language. However, John did something completely unexpected: he put his ear down to the book, screwed up his face, looked up and said, 'I can't hear what she's saying!' Although very amusing, you can see how such a reply would not be considered either appropriate or usual. In fact it borders on the bizarre.

We use many procedures for testing, too numerous to mention, but one particular assessment is worth describing, simply because it is so widely used for children up to the age of seven years. Called the 'Reynell Developmental Language Scales', it is used to assess both a child's understanding and his use of language through the natural medium of play. From the therapist's point of view, it is easy to administer and likely to keep a child's attention because of the attractive toys, which vary as the assessment proceeds. It is divided into two major sections, one to assess the understanding of language and the other the use of language; both are designed to follow the stages of language development. For example, each of the subsections which deal with language understanding is slightly harder than the previous one: language ranges from labelling—'Show me the table'—to complex language such as 'Put all the animals in this box, except the black pig.'

The section dealing with language use assesses a child's vocabulary—the ability to explain what words mean. For example, he might be asked, 'What is "cold"?' It also looks at how children use language in sentences—how long the sentences are, the number of ideas they contain, and the diversity of grammar used.

We are all too aware that no one test will give a complete picture of a child's speech and language skills, it is only a part of it. Assessment is rather like assembling a jigsaw. Everything you, as parents, tell us, gives us more pieces of the jigsaw; add to it our own observations and test results and possibly any information from other professionals involved, and hopefully we shall have the complete picture.

As I mentioned previously, you can see how important parents are to the process of assessment, for without your co-operation we could easily reach the wrong conclusion. Sometimes the whole procedure can take as long as an hour, but if the problem is a complex one it may require several visits. So much depends on the co-operation of your child. In fact, assessment doesn't cease after the first visit; therapy is used as an opportunity to gain further insight into a child's problems.

The range of problems we see in the local clinic is enormous, from simple lisps to very severe and specific speech and language disorder. Lee, aged four years, was an example of a fairly obvious problem. The day I met him, his mother dragged him screaming into the room and, apparently, for him this behaviour was not unusual. She told me that he had always been a difficult child and nothing would pacify him. Unable to tolerate the tantrums any longer, she took the least line of resistance and plonked a dummy into his mouth. Because the dummy was the one thing that calmed him this was what she had always done, so it was not surprising that Lee had learned to speak with a dummy permanently in his mouth. All his speech was articulated at the back of his mouth. Pinned down at the front, only the back half of his tongue could move with any degree of ease, so that every time he wanted to make a sound normally made at the front of the mouth, such as a 't' or 'd', he was forced to make a 'k' or 'g'. Lip sounds, such as 'm', 'p' and 'b', were of course out of the question. The remediation was quite simple: remove the dummy and the child's speech would, with a little help, improve.

Martin's problems were rather more serious. At the age of three he appeared to have no meaningful understanding of what was said to him; he could not even select one of his favourite toys when asked to do so. He echoed much of what was said to him, but appeared unable to produce meaningful speech. By observing him it was noticed that he made sense of the world through visual means, through routines and context. Unlike Lee, Martin had a severe and complex language problem which required many years of therapy. He needed structured teaching at first, to improve his understanding, whilst at the same time we took every opportunity to expand his use of language. As he grew older it was possible to work on more specific aspects of language—for example, verb tense, plural nouns, pronouns—until he had progressed enough to be discharged from therapy.

Children who stammer are always treated as urgent cases. It has been found that early preventative work with parents, as soon as the stammer is noticed, is often the key to preventing a stammer continuing into adulthood. Voice problems are rare, but when they occur we always first seek advice from an ENT consultant, for there could be a more sinister reason than the usual straightforward misuse and abuse of voice and, although extremely rare in children, there might be a cancerous growth. With this particular condition we can never be too careful.

Oral Examination

The experience of peering inside any child's mouth can be full of surprises and quite hazardous: there are sneezes, coughs and even bites to be wary of. So what is the reason for pursuing this seemingly perilous course? It is necessary for the therapist to examine lips, tongue, teeth, tonsils and soft palate—that's the bit that moves up and down at the back of your mouth when you say 'ah'—to ascertain that everything is in place and working correctly. I have seen tonsils so enormous you wonder how a child could possibly move her tongue, and imagine how alarming it is for a therapist to find an almost toothless child, at the age of five! With the increasing education on the AIDS virus and the dangers of hepatitis, it is vital nowadays, when examining the insides of children's mouths, to use spatulas and rubber gloves.

After Assessment

Whilst assessing a child, the therapist will intuitively have various ideas about the kind of difficulty your child might be experiencing and the possible causes. In medical language this process is called a 'differential diagnosis', and when you go to the doctor with a pain in your stomach, she will go through a similar process. She may, from her questions, have a fairly good idea what the problem might be, then by various tests and her own examination come to a conclusion. Therapists are no different, as Figure 3 shows.

At the conclusion of the assessment your therapist will summarise her observations and test results for you. All therapists make every effort to use terms you will understand, but from time to time we are all fallible and may occasionally slip into 'therapy speak'. If you don't understand, never be afraid to ask.

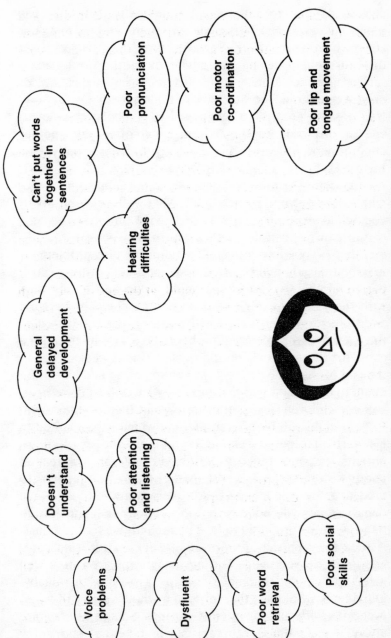

Figure 3. Thoughts running through a speech and language therapist's mind when assessing a child—What's wrong and why?

Most parents are desperate to know why their child has a particular speech or language problem: sadly, we do not always have the answer. Sometimes we may suspect what the cause might be, but the advice of another professional such as an educational psychologist or clinical medical officer may be sought before we consider undertaking any therapy. It is possible that the assessment has not been completed, and in this instance the therapist will offer you another appointment for your child, usually fairly promptly (see Figure 4).

Next, your therapist will discuss a 'programme of management': quite simply, this means what will be done about your child's problem. It may be advice on what you as a parent can do, coupled with a return review visit in a few months, or possibly longer depending on the problem. It may be that you will be offered an appointment for a block period of therapy. Most therapists enter into a 'contract' with the 'client's carer'. In this case the client is the child and the undertaking will be with yourself, the parent, called the client's carer. You will probably be asked to attend the clinic for therapy for a period of six to eight weeks, then at the end of this time progress will be reviewed and a decision made in discussion with parents, on what will be done next.

Some children work better in a group than on their own, so your child will be offered therapy which is best suited to his particular personality and problem, and at all times parents are encouraged to participate. We are aware that parents often make the best therapists, so be prepared to take an active role in your child's therapy at the clinic. Some departments will operate a more intensive approach to therapy, so be prepared to take your child two to three times a week for a period of six or eight weeks, after which progress will be reviewed. During the groups, you may well meet speech and language therapy assistants, invaluable individuals who assist therapists in a whole variety of ways, especially with running intensive groups. School holidays are always a hectic time for therapists, who take the opportunity

Figure 4. Programme of management: or what will be done about your child's problem.

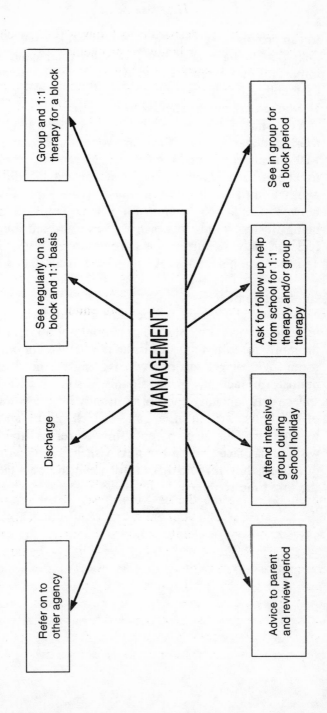

to run groups of varying kinds, usually welcomed by parents delighted to have added activities for their children. It is important that parents should also be prepared to work with their children at home, to reinforce the work of the therapist and ensure as rapid progress as possible.

You should be aware of the policy adopted by most therapy departments with regard to non-attendance. If you wish to cancel an appointment for any reason, do please let us know, or it is quite likely that you will not be offered another until we hear from you. At the rate of anything between £30 to £40 per hour for a therapist, NHS funds are being wasted, funds to which we have all contributed. We feel it is only a courtesy for parents not to waste our time and the nation's money. A 'phone call is all that is needed.

Information Sheets

How many times have we been to a doctor who has given us advice on what we should or should not do, and we have promptly forgotten most of it the minute we got outside the room. We all get anxious when going to the doctor, the dentist, in fact any professional person. Aware of this, speech and language therapists usually have a whole range of handouts, written in language which can be understood by anyone. This gives parents time to reflect, think about what took place and on the next visit be ready with all the questions they forgot, or did not have the courage to ask the first time round.

2 Language And Its Problems

Disbelief is usually the first emotion felt by parents when they realise that there is something amiss with their child's speech and language development. Along with this comes an array of other emotions: guilt, panic, anxiety and sometimes denial. Most parents begin asking themselves what they have done wrong or what they have forgotten to do. Have they talked to their child too infrequently or been absent at crucial times? Have they perhaps talked too much, not allowing time for their child's responses?

Language is such an important part of our lives, and yet, as with many other skills, we do not truly appreciate this fact until something goes wrong. No wonder, as parents, you become alarmed when your child shows every sign of not developing language at the right time and in the right way.

Parents have sometimes said to me that their child cannot communicate properly, and when questioned further it emerges that they are referring to a lack of language, not the whole range of abilities which relate to language.

We do need to be aware of other abilities which relate to language, interact with it, but are not exactly the same. Frequently we use the terms 'language', 'speech' and 'communication' as if they had precisely the same meaning, but in fact they are not synonymous and it is helpful to know and understand the differences between them. Language can be defined in many ways and the following is one of them: 'It is a shared system of verbal symbols and rules, that allows us to communicate with others. It is arbitrary, creative and learned.' So what does all this mean? 'Verbal symbols' are the words or building blocks of language, and the way in which we use them to represent the world around us demonstrates most obviously the arbitrary nature of language. For example, a four-legged animal which 'miaows' is called 'cat' in English and *chat* in French. There appears to be no particular, logical or essential relationship between the word and what it actually represents. You could just as easily call it a 'fug'. It is only a 'cat' or *chat* because everyone who speaks English or French agrees that these words represent four-legged animals that 'miaow'.

Language abounds with rules. There are rules of grammar, rules on how sounds fit together in words, rules on how the meanings of words and sentences change, depending on the way we use them, rules which govern how we use language for the many differing situations we encounter in everyday life. Language is creative because users can actually create and understand sentences they have never heard before. It's amazing, isn't it, that with a finite set of symbols (words) and rules, we can produce an infinite number of sentences. There is just one small catch, though: it all has to be learned. Everyone in the language community must learn the symbols and rules of their native language, in order that they can communicate with one another.

Speech is the oral expression of language, and if you ever thought patting your head and rubbing your tummy was a complicated act to do, stop for a moment to ponder on how incredibly complicated it is to produce speech. Speaking involves a complex set of actions by various muscles which are needed to produce sound sequences that can be understood by others. The basic 'units' of speech are speech sounds and these are combined to form 'language units', such as words and sentences. The melodies and rhythms we use to express these words and sentences add both meaning and colour to our language. It really is an amazing feat for children to be able to deal with the demands of learning speech and language simultaneously.

Although speech seems to be the most widely used and, some might say, the most efficient way of expressing language in our society, it is by no means the only one. One of the most common alternatives is writing, but there are other ways by which we can convey our thoughts, feelings and messages. Deaf people, for instance, use manual signing, and there are other non-speech modes of communicating which will be discussed in later chapters. So you see, not all language—and by this I mean language in its broadest context—is necessarily spoken language.

While communication encompasses both speech and language, it is a much more general type of behaviour, which involves the way we share thoughts, ideas, attitudes and feelings with others. Communication is what speech and language are about, but we must remember that we can also communicate without either of these. Music, art, theatre, facial expression, body posture and gesture are all forms of communication, even though they do not involve verbal symbols. Young children can communicate long before they are able to produce any intelligible words. Do you recall your baby stretching up his or her arms to be picked up, and your immediate response? Communication of this kind, in normally developing children, comes before the development of speech and language.

Normal Development
Terms such as 'normal' or 'average' are used all the time in relation to the pattern of development we see in children. Normal development has a time frame associated with it, so that, for the most part, we have a fairly good idea of what children should be doing at a particular age. In real life there are fairly wide variations within what we would accept as being 'normal', and language, as with other developments, goes through well documented stages. We are all aware of those children, thankfully few in number, who have disabilities which are apparent at birth, or soon after; they are

considered 'at risk' and may not develop language, speech, even communication in the normal way.

Therapists are frequently asked what signs mothers should be looking for before seeking help: our usual response is, as soon as you notice something is wrong, either in a child's understanding or in his use of language. In my experience, most mothers are very perceptive about their children. They notice how and when their children respond; they are always observing differences between their Suzie and Jamie next door. Children vary so much in the rate at which they acquire language that we hesitate to be too dogmatic about what is, or is not, a problem. As a general rule, it is time to be concerned when intuitively you feel your child should be talking. Again, you might also notice that he is not understanding, not responding as he should. Don't be afraid to seek help. It may be that he is not hearing you. On the other hand, language may be developing very well, and yet you still can't understand a word your child is saying, because many speech sounds are missing or replaced by others. Most children should have acquired some words by the age of 18 months and have begun using short sentences by the age of three years. Other aspects of communication, like fluency or voice, can sometimes be affected.

Our general advice is: be concerned earlier rather than later. Children who have any of these difficulties may well experience a wide range of emotional, social and learning problems. We must constantly be aware that a small unresolved difficulty could, in time, develop into a real humdinger of a problem. Children can differ so much in their acceptance of their problems; some may become so frustrated that their behaviour deteriorates and they become aggressive and uncontrollable, or the opposite occurs and they may become very withdrawn. Others accept their burden with amazing tolerance. What is surprising is, quite simply, that the degree of disturbance does not always relate to the severity of the problem.

The Size of the Problem

Over the years, studies have been undertaken to ascertain how many children in the population have speech and language difficulties; the trouble with studies of this kind is how to decide who has a problem and how it should be measured. A particularly awesome piece of research took place in 1958, when it was decided to follow the development of a group of children throughout the land, who had been born in the same week. This of course included observing their speech and language. As you can imagine, with such a vast undertaking, findings varied. According to the medical officers, from a sample of 15,000 children, 14 per cent had some kind of speech problem, whilst teachers, on the other hand, found only 11 per cent. Whatever the overall conclusions, it would appear that there are times when even the professionals have difficulty in defining what constitutes a problem.

Further studies over the years have experienced similar problems, but Dr David Crystal, the prolific writer, broadcaster and academic, suggests that around an alarming ten per cent of the nation's children have a language handicap severe enough to be a problem both to themselves and to the people who look after them—and this he considers a conservative estimate. Apply this statistic to ordinary schools and we find that about two to three children in every class will have a greater or lesser degree of language impairment. What a daunting prospect for the poor teachers, who may have over thirty children in their classes, including some with other kinds of disability. And this is not the complete story: we must not forget that 40 per cent of children attending special schools will need therapy at some time during their school life. These two salient statistics alone show that some courageous decisions have to be made if we are to preserve the well-being of the nation's children.

HOW LANGUAGE DEVELOPS

In the space of a few short years the early cries of babies develop into coherent speech. Equally amazing is how mothers and fathers interpret what to the rest of us sounds like incomprehensible babble. Little Johnny has just said 'ba da da da', which is instantly interpreted as 'Oh, he says he wants a drinkie'. There is, we know, a very serious aspect of parents giving meaning to whatever baby is saying, claiming as they do to understand every little smile, gesture and mood. In those first few weeks of a baby's life mothers establish a pattern of communication with their children by touching, smiling, looking and talking. Experiences are shared by mother and child. She communicates by the tone of her voice and by gestures, as well as by speech. So the early seeds of communication are sown between mother and child.

Parents, especially mothers, unconsciously adapt their speech and language to that of their child. In a strange sort of way, they always seem to be in tune, one small step ahead, whilst at the same time keeping their child's attention and making sure they are understood. At some time or other, most of us have entered into 'baby talk', knowing we are catching the child's attention, making friends and, hopefully, being understood.

Babies respond to all this kind of behaviour and gradually begin to communicate with their mothers. Because they learn language so easily and with such incredible speed, it is generally accepted that children must have some inborn ability to acquire language. They are born, it seems, with the urge to communicate, in order that they can learn about the world. Throughout life we strive to have friends and be accepted by others, to become members of a family, our workplace and society.

If asked when you thought your child began to talk, like most other parents, you would probably say he was about one year old when he spoke his first real words. In fact it doesn't just happen overnight, like magic; a child doesn't just wake up one morning and is talking. To have reached this stage, rather like making a cake, all the ingredients have taken time to be put together before it is baked. Language acquisition begins at birth and, some may say, even before this. From birth babies prefer and distinguish their own mothers' voices from other female voices: there is a substantial body of opinion which suggests that a new-born baby recognises its mother's voice because it was able to hear it before birth, whilst in its mother's womb. New-born babies also prefer human speech over all kinds of other sounds, including instrumental or vocal music.

The First Year of Life
In learning to communicate we all need to have certain abilities, and perhaps the most obvious of these is being able to make speech sounds and string them together in a way to make understandable words. It is also essential to be able to perceive those sounds and make sense of what someone is saying to you and, finally, to be able to have a conversation and communicate in every way with other people.

During this first year of life, the child goes through various recognisable stages of sounds before anything emerges that is vaguely speechlike and resembles a word. You may hear a number of the 46 or so speech sounds distinctive to the English language, but don't expect miracles, for he has a way to go yet. Early sounds are few—mainly burping and sneezing, coughing and, on occasions, being sick! By about two months these sounds begin to change and give way to vowel-like sounds which we call cooing—comfort-like sounds usually produced in response to Mum's or Dad's smiling and talking. Even at this early stage it is possible to hear the odd consonant sound. Different cries can be identified between four and five months and laughter appears at about the same time. By five to six months, babies produce vocal play, sequences of vowel and consonant sounds which merge into babbling, perhaps one of the most distinctive stages of the first year of life.

Help Me Speak

Babies appear to take great pleasure in repeating these strings of consonants and vowels, such as 'ba ba ba', 'da da da'. These continue to be used well into the second year of life and grow increasingly complex as the melodies and rhythms of this babbling begin to resemble what therapists know as 'chunks' of speech. It often sounds so speech-like, we feel we really should be understanding it. At this stage, my niece would produce a whole string of babble, what is termed 'variegated babble', and would then look at me expectantly, as if waiting for an answer. The problem was that none of this baby babble was ever intelligible. Even so, I felt guilty because I had not understood, as if I should have done but had not really tried hard enough. At about one year that magical first word appears, but it is only regarded as a real word when its sound and meaning both become clear.

We must not forget that children are able to communicate with other people around them, and understand what communication is all about, at an early stage. For example, when an infant cries, mum usually reacts by picking him up, feeding or changing him. This early behaviour develops and by nine to ten months is becoming intentional. At this stage there are two principal ways in which babies specifically communicate their needs, and these appear at about the same time as they begin to use words. One is to call the attention of a parent, usually the mother, to an object or an event, typically by pointing or giving an object to her. The other is the regulation of people's behaviour by either gesturing or vocalising to get mum, or whoever in the family is nearby, to do what baby wants.

Parents, whilst reacting to the overall communication attempts of their child, have by now tuned in to the increasing variations of melody, rhythm and tone, sense the intention behind these utterances and attribute meaning to them, often correctly; they recognise when it is a question, when they are being called, greeted or being told baby wants something.

From experiments which have been carried out, there is more to young babies than we have previously been led to believe. They have the ability, it would appear, to discriminate between various pairs of consonants or vowels—for example, 'pa' from 'ba'—from as early as four weeks of age. At the moment, no one really knows whether this is an ability specific to human beings or whether it might be shared by certain other animals (chinchillas and rhesus monkeys have shown comparable responses).

When they are a year old, babies can understand anything from 20 to 60 words, although they are not yet able to say all these. During a baby's first year of life, everyone in the family is there at its beck and call, and all the time the child is assimilating language. Apply this to yourself and imagine the benefits of learning a foreign language, when throughout the day you are surrounded by people speaking to you in the language you wish to learn. With that kind of non-stop, undivided attention, you will soon acquire a great deal of that language. So it is with our year-old babe.

The Second Year
From the beginning of the second year most children produce their first recognisable words, but these may not sound exactly like the way you and I say them, although as children's language progresses, towards the end of the second year when word linking has emerged, you will probably be able to identify your child using up to 20 different speech sounds.

All this is no accident, for children's speech follows a clear sequence of development. You'll hear very few hissy sounds like 'f', 's' and 'sh'; these are usually replaced by an explosive sort of sound such as 't' and 'k'—'sea', for example, becomes 'tea'. At this stage, children prefer sounds at the front of their mouth to those at the back, so 'car' becomes 'tar'. Clusters of sounds such as 'st' or 'tr' are really hard to say, so 'star' becomes 'tar', and 'tree', 'tea'. They will also make sounds match or harmonise with one another, especially with longer

words, so 'table' become 'bable'. Consonant sounds are usually pronounced at the beginning of words and left off at the
end, so 'horse' becomes 'hor'. Then there are long words
with lots of syllables, difficult to pronounce anyway, which
are said with quiet bits or whole syllables missed out. One
we all know is 'nana' for 'banana'. Variations of pronunciation are normal, so don't be surprised if you hear the same
word produced in many different ways.

Throughout life, we always understand more words than
we actually use; as adults, for every word we use we understand three or four more. Babies at 18 months can be
expected to say about 50 words, but equally important is
that they can understand anything between 150–200 words
relating to their immediate environment, to actions, locations, social words, describing words, and 'empty' words like
'thing', 'one' and 'there'.

Now we come to a fascinating aspect of this stage in development: how children use one word to mean a whole host
of things. It is called 'overextension'. One common example
is how children use 'dog' to refer not only to dogs, but to
all four-legged animals; more embarrassing for mothers is
when every male in sight is referred to as 'dada'! The opposite, referred to as 'underextension', also occurs. Some years
ago, I recall my nephew using the word 'car' to refer to his
toy car, but when asked about the family's car or other cars,
he hadn't the slightest idea what they were called. Children
use their repertoire of single words to great effect, communicating a variety of intentions such as: naming objects, repeating words, answering questions, greeting people, in general
protesting, and those oh so endless repetitions.

When the young child is approaching 18 months, the stage
at which words are beginning to be linked, you will notice
a steady stream of words popping up again and again. Some
of the most popular and frequently used are 'all gone', 'gone'
and 'more'. The ever popular 'Daddy gone', as most of you
will know, can mean 'he's gone', as a statement of the obvious, but as far as the child is concerned it could also be a

question. On the other hand, it could just as easily be a command: 'All right, Dad's gone, so let's get on with my dinner, please.' It is fascinating that, even though there are only two words, the order in which they are used usually follows what you would expect to hear from an adult sentence. You usually hear 'my doll' not 'doll my', and 'got that', not 'that got'. Some children even get as far as using verbs with '-ing' endings like 'running' and 'walking', or 's' to indicate more than one thing.

The Third and Fourth Years
In two short years our gurgling baby has grown beyond all recognition. Gone are the bubbles and burping; now he is putting words together, and the greatest fun of all for everyone is being able to have a conversation. By the third year, as Dr Crystal says, the proverbial duckling will have become a swan. Don't bother to start counting numbers of words, there will be just too many of them. By now words and phrases will be popping out every few seconds. It is always a problem to know what to count, because one word can have a variety of meanings. 'Turn' alone can mean 'turn over', 'turn out', 'take a turn', 'turn something', 'turn in' (for the night). At the same time sentences become longer, considerably longer, using more complex grammar. So instead of 'cat go bed', each bit of the sentence is expanded to 'that cat going in bed'. At this time children also learn about word endings such as '-er', '-est' '-ing', but don't always use them correctly at this stage. You might hear such phrases as 'he's biggerer than me', or 'I wanting that'.

Ask any parents what they remember about their three-year-old, and the answer will undoubtedly be, the never-ending questions. No doubt the following conversation, or something like this, will bring back memories to many mothers:

Gavin, aged three years and one month
G: Where's your hair, Mummy?

M: I had it cut.
G: Why cut?
M: Because it was long.
G: Why long?
M: Well, because it grows.
G: Why it grow, Mummy?
M: Because God made it grow.
G: Why God made it grow?

You can hear the exasperation beginning to creep into Mum's voice and, believe me, the 'why' stage of questioning can seem endless.

To be able to cope with all this extra complicated language, far more speech sounds have appeared and are used in a more accurate way. But don't expect to hear the more difficult sounds like 'sh', 'ch' or 'r'. How many times have I heard parents complaining that their three-and-a-half year-old isn't using his 'r' correctly, or can't say 'splash' yet. Although by now many children will have sorted out 't' and 'k', many more will still be saying 'tea' for 'key' or 'tar' for 'car'.

With great gusto, conversation will have begun to take off. One anxious mother I knew was dismayed that her son was not speaking as expected at the age of two-and-a-half years. She was just as dismayed when, at three-and-a-half years, he was asking endless questions, disagreeing, making comments, in fact, chattering away like a little chipmunk. Some parents are never content with their child's development.

Don't be alarmed if, during this explosion of language, your child develops what may sound like a stammer, what therapists refer to as a dysfluency. At this time children have so much to say, they are just so excited by the world around them, that they often repeat, hesitate, get stuck, and take long pauses. Not all children will go through this, but many do and it's nothing to get too worried about. It will much more likely become a problem if you consider it to be one, and make your child feel it is one.

Four Years Onwards

Language continues to develop at a fair rate during four years and five years, depending on the child; some will make more progress than others, for the exact pace of language development is always difficult to predetermine. Apart from the vocabulary, which continues to expand, and the many new meanings of words children must learn, perhaps one of the hardest aspects a child has to conquer is grammar, with all its pitfalls and irregularities. Words such as 'if', 'so', 'while', 'but', 'because' begin to be used in the right way, to make more complex and colourful sentences. Again Dr Crystal observes that by now it seems a lifetime away from 'car' to 'my daddy took the car so we could get there quick'. Of course there will still be errors, but they have only become more noticeable because everything else that is said sounds so good. And as for speech sounds, well, a few will remain problematical, but we would hardly consider them errors as such, for we don't expect children to have mastered everything just yet. The consonants 'r' and 's' can present difficulties, and so can the more complicated sound clusters like 'spr' or 'squ', but fortunately the rest are in place to cope with the flow of language which, like a miracle, has appeared in so short a time. In the years since birth children have learned to be successful communicators and acquired many of the social graces; without these skills entry into school is indeed a worrisome prospect.

LANGUAGE PROBLEMS

For most children, learning language is a reasonably easy, problem-free exercise. Language for them is fulfilling and pleasurable, following a fairly predictable path of development. Some, regretfully, are not so lucky. For them, the path to language learning is fraught with difficulties, and for their parents it is a time of great anxiety.

The kind of problems which children experience in learning language, learning to speak and learning to communicate fall into several broad areas and, all too often, parents can become confused by the terms professionals use to describe them. Recent figures showed that something like fifty are in current use. Many of the terms refer to the same kind of problem, but why should you, the parents, necessarily be aware of this? Terms can be helpful if we all know what they mean and they are clearly explained. For this reason, at the end of the book I have included a glossary of terms which you might hear when your child is being discussed.

Broadly speaking, difficulties fall into two main areas— input and output. It is always helpful to use the analogy of yourself learning another language: the difference in this situation is that you have already learned your native language and so have some idea of what constitutes a language and how you use it to make people understand. Young children don't start out having this particular advantage. They are, as it were, starting at the beginning.

Input Problems
What is it that we find problematical about learning another language? To begin with, words themselves are essential. If you don't have sufficient vocabulary—names of objects, action words, words for feelings, positions, descriptions, concepts, and all those difficult 'little' words which are the cement of language—you will not understand what is being said. Not knowing a word, just one, is enough, and whilst you are desperately trying to work out what it means, you completely miss everything that follows. Faced with this, you may well misunderstand what has been said, reply inappropriately, and do the wrong thing. To my intense embarrassment, whilst on holiday in France, I confused *deux heures* (two o'clock) and *douze heures* (twelve o'clock) and arrived two hours late for lunch!

With grammar, it is essential to learn the rules, there's just no getting away from it. Rules need to be learned in such a way that they become second nature; it is not sufficient to memorise one or two, because to master understanding you need to be able to grasp all of them. When you hear the sentence 'the boy chasing the dog is fat', you need to be able to decide who is fat. Is it the boy or is it the dog? And what about all those speech sounds? You need to be able to remember what they sound like, how you make them, and how one change of sound can completely change the meaning of a word. Not only that, it is also essential to detect subtle differences between speech sounds. In my own case, had I not been on the telephone, undoubtedly my trained ear would have noticed the difference between *deux* and *douze*. Speech sounds come in sequences, some never appearing next to others in a word. In English you will never find an 's' and 'j' together at the beginning of a word, or words ending with certain short vowel sounds. Once again there are rules to be learned, in this instance on how speech sounds are organised in words.

We need to be aware that it is not only *what* is said to you, but *how* it is said, that can totally change meaning. Consider a blackboard and a black board: they obviously have different meanings, each referring to a different object. The tunes of our language also need to be learned, and they are different from those of other languages and if not learned correctly can interfere with how others understand us. We have probably all had experience of trying to understand someone from China, for example, who may have a wonderful grasp of our language but hasn't learned the right intonation patterns. Exactly the same thing happens if we cannot easily learn the tunes of our own language.

Once we have mastered content, grammar and speech sounds, we are then faced with perhaps one of the hardest aspects of language, the meaning behind the meaning—you know, the 'nod, nod, wink, wink' kind of language we all appreciate. In every language, colloquial and idiomatic expressions can bring about a glazed look or one of incredulity—for example, when you hear, 'I've had my nose down all weekend'. Even more bizarre are the phrases from a specific group like the Navy, such as, 'let's jack it in', which broadly translated means, 'let's forget the job in hand and get out of here'. Then there's the metaphor: children can produce some hilarious metaphors without realising it. One child I recall described a man shaving as 'giving his face a haircut'. Finally we come to a really difficult area: jokes, sarcasm and irony are, from my point of view, the hardest kind of language for any child to understand; adults, let alone children, are at times oblivious of them.

If you are trying to translate a sentence from a foreign language into English, and can only rely on finding the meaning of each separate word in a dictionary, you will soon realise that the sentence as a whole has more meaning than all the individual words within it. It is no different in our own language, for sentences have their own meanings. Sooner or later we also have to learn the rules, or what are currently called protocols, of conversation making—understanding when it is time to talk or not talk, to interrupt, change a topic and, of equal importance, when to terminate a conversation. Quite simply, if a child has difficulty in understanding any of the aspects of language which I have just described, most likely his responses will be incoherent.

Output Problems
It is all too apparent that language is littered with rules which need to be understood and learned: if you cannot grasp these rules, it is unlikely that you will be able to put them into practice in speech, whether in French, Chinese or your mother tongue. You need to have understood for example, that in English an adjective (a describing word, such as 'red') always comes before a noun, whereas in French it usually comes after. You will know from learning any foreign language how complicated grammar can be, and however well you have understood the rules, it is not always so easy to apply them when you are talking.

Equally, unless you have understood the rules that decide how sounds are organised in words, those sounds will come out in a jumbled up way when you speak (see Figure 5).

Figure 5.

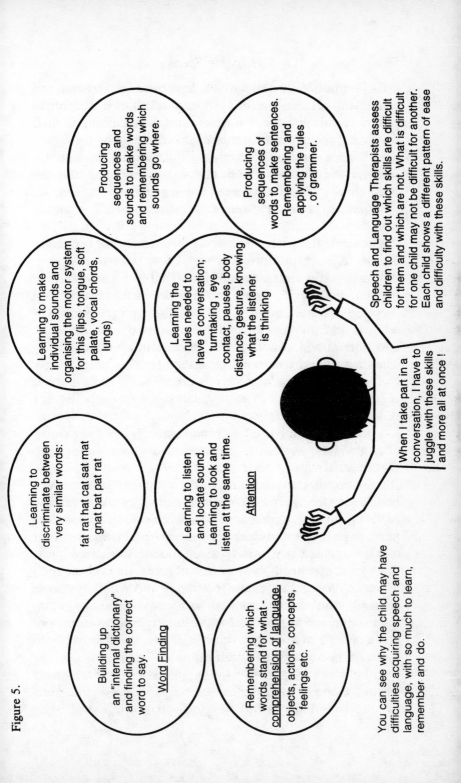

Producing sequences and sounds to make words and remembering which sounds go where.

Producing sequences of words to make sentences. Remembering and applying the rules of grammer.

Learning to make individual sounds and organising the motor system for this (lips, tongue, soft palate, vocal chords, lungs)

Learning the rules needed to have a conversation; turntaking , eye contact, pauses, body distance, gesture, knowing what the listener is thinking

Learning to discriminate between very similar words:

fat rat hat cat sat mat gnat bat pat rat

Learning to listen and locate sound. Learning to look and listen at the same time.

Attention

Building up an "internal dictionary" and finding the correct word to say.

Word Finding

Remembering which words stand for what - comprehension of language: objects, actions, concepts, feelings etc.

When I take part in a conversation, I have to juggle with these skills and more all at once !

Speech and Language Therapists assess children to find out which skills are difficult for them and which are not. What is difficult for one child may not be difficult for another. Each child shows a different pattern of ease and difficulty with these skills.

You can see why the child may have difficulties acquiring speech and language, with so much to learn, remember and do.

Sometimes, even though you have managed to come to terms with all these rules, you may still find it difficult to put them into practice. Understanding is one thing, doing is another. Speech can be unintelligible not only because children cannot remember the rules of pronunciation, but also because they cannot physically make, sequence and co-ordinate the fine and complex movements of their tongue, lips, palate, larynx and lungs, in order to produce speech sounds.

The strategies we learn to enable us to have conversations also need to be put into practice. These skills develop significantly between the ages of three and five when children become increasingly aware of the social factors that govern successful conversation—such as the correct forms of address and markers of politeness (for example, 'please', and 'sorry') and how to make requests in an indirect way. The art of good conversation, no matter how old you are, is crucial for everyday living; without the skill of putting these rules into practice, individuals can very easily become isolated and misunderstood.

Vocabulary can be just as problematical. Knowing words does not mean you can instantly retrieve them for your 'lexicon' or word store, at the exact moment when you want them. Remember that awful occasion when you met someone you hadn't seen for ages? You went through all the usual 'hellos', realising with increasing horror that you couldn't remember her name. It can and does happen over and over again for children, on a daily, hourly, even minute-to-minute basis. They know the words but just cannot access them at the right moment. We all know how frustrating and pointless it is to remember the word we wanted, half-an-hour after the event.

In conversation it is most important to produce appropriate language at the right time, and also to respond with the right non-verbal communication. A smile at the wrong moment can wreck a conversation, just as easily as the wrong words. To be able to participate fully, we must eventually acquire the ability to use language in a subtle and more sophisticated way, or we shall spend our time discussing the obvious and the literal.

Children can have difficulties with any aspect of output, and these can be compounded by lack of fluency in the form of a stammer (more commonly referred to nowadays by therapists as a 'dysfluency'), or by problems with voice. Children have so much to do and remember when they talk that it is a miracle they ever manage to say anything.

Causes of Speech and Language Difficulties
Sooner or later, the majority of parents I have worked with over the years want to know what has caused their child's language problem, unless of course the cause, such as a physical disability, has been obvious from birth. Sometimes, with the help of other professionals, we are able to identify one or more factors which would have caused the problem, but irrespective of the progress in research, in many cases we have to be honest and admit we do not have an answer.

There is a baffling and often heated debate among professionals today, concerning the use of labels when referring to those of us who are not able-bodied. Some consider labels offensive and irrelevant, since they tell us about a disability, not about a person: surely it is society's perception that is wrong, if a person with a disability is considered to be 'handicapped'. Again, this view is reflected in the use of the term 'special needs', which encompasses every child or adult who in some way or other requires extra help to learn and live.

Most parents would not disagree with this, but from experience I know that they really do appreciate a label that helps them understand and come to terms with their child's disability. It is most important to remember that a label is not a permanent fixture, or for that matter a stigma, and it certainly does not necessarily give us any idea of the degree of the problem.

Hearing loss is an example, since it is one of the first causes that we might consider when a child is referred for a speech and language therapy assessment. It can be an intermittent loss which, with drugs or a simple operation, can be resolved. On the other hand, it might be of a more permanent nature, and could make a significant difference to the child's life, because of the detrimental effect it has on his ability to learn, which of course includes language and speech. Conceivably it may require some kind of specialist educational provision; but even so, the term itself tells us very little about the individual's difficulties or his special needs.

Physical disability is a very obvious cause of a speech and language impairment, which is often sustained at or around birth but can occur at any time. It is an all-encompassing term for every type of physical disability, but almost everyone will be familiar with the term 'cerebral palsy', which is caused by damage to or underdevelopment of the brain and is a condition which affects control of movement. It is not a single disorder, but a variety of conditions. Diseases, accidents and syndromes can equally be the cause of brain damage or muscular deterioration, at any time in our lives, and children are certainly not exempt from these conditions.

Structural Problems
One of the best known 'structural' problems is cleft lip and palate, but there are other types of deformity which can interfere with speech development.

One of the main reasons for operating on cleft lip and palate is so that the child will eventually be able to learn to speak, for unless this is done he has no way of forming the sounds of our language accurately. There is no effective seal or division between nose and mouth, and no gum ridge to use. Although day-to-day living will have its restrictions and a degree of frustration, it is possible to live without operating. Feeding can be a problem if no surgery is undertaken, but the condition is not usually life-threatening. Another very obvious but less frequent reason for speech difficulties is a lack of teeth. Fortunately, with the dental care programme available nowadays, this is a rare occurrence.

Learning Difficulty

Put simply, when we talk about learning difficulty we mean that children have difficulty with some, or in some cases all, aspects of learning. Three most frequently used terms are specific, moderate and severe learning difficulty. Specific learning difficulty implies that one or more crucial areas of learning are affected, whilst others remain unimpaired. Moderate and severe learning difficulties imply that all aspects of learning are affected to a greater or lesser degree. Throughout, many children will experience difficulty in learning language, but parents must not be alarmed by this, for therapists are very aware that this is by no means an unusual occurrence.

Most of you will be familiar with the condition known as Down's Syndrome. Many children who have this condition will have learning difficulties, with problems in learning language and speech. There are many more lesser known and rarer syndromes which may also have an effect on development. Children with physical disability can also experience learning difficulties, which in turn affect their speech and language development.

Emotional Trauma and Behavioural Problems

Whilst we recognise that all families experience the usual ups and downs of daily living, there are some which stumble from crisis to crisis. In these families, we must not always assume that a family crisis, no matter how frequent, will have a lasting psychological effect on the child. However, when these circumstances do exist there is every likelihood that children may be deprived of the usual nurturing. Physical abuse, sexual abuse, neglect, psychological cruelty are all factors which are detrimental to all developments. Children react in different ways to deprivation and abuse: some withdraw, many develop behaviour problems. Other traumas such as bereavement, families splitting up, even illness, can be equally destructive to language development.

Autism

From time to time we see reports in the newspapers or on TV about children who are autistic. They have been described as living in a world of their own, seemingly unable to make sense of the world around them and especially the people in it. They have a communication difficulty in which language plays a part, since it is one of the means by which we make contact with and make sense of people and the world. Children with autism, whether their condition is mild or severe, do not easily understand language and have great difficulty using it in a communicative way.

Developmental Delay

This relates to children aged two to three years or younger, who are delayed in various developmental milestones, and it is not unusual for language to be one of them. We don't always know why this delay occurs, but occasionally the reason may be apparent, as, for example, in children who are born prematurely. Very often children with these kinds of delay at an early stage in their life are found, later, to have learning difficulties.

Feeding Difficulties

Although it doesn't happen very often, some children have great difficulty in feeding; they sometimes cannot suck, chew or swallow in the usual way. The problem can be apparent even when they are babies, in children with physical disability, various syndromes, degenerative diseases and structural abnormalities. The analogy is a broad one; however, we can say that feeding is to speech as crawling is to walking: unless you master one, you are unlikely to progress easily to the other.

Several Languages

Many children are brought up in homes where several languages are spoken, and for most of them this has no effect on their ability to speak English. However, if parents do not speak English themselves, then their children will need to be taught it as soon as possible, in order to learn in school. In parts of the country where there are large immigrant groups, there are excellent programmes to deal with the problems posed by English as a second language. The children referred to therapists, however, are those who do not seem to be learning any language adequately, not even the one spoken in the home. In these cases we can only assume that the second or third language is a complicating factor, and that the children would find language difficult to learn whatever their circumstances.

Some parents may well be thinking, 'But none of this applies to our child', and they would not be wrong. Along with these parents we feel dissatisfied that, irrespective of our years of experience and the vast amounts of research undertaken into the subject, we still do not always know what causes speech and language difficulties in some children. We are hopeful that, as our knowledge and understanding increase of one of the most complex of human behaviours, we shall, one day, have the answers.

3 Specialist Help Pre-School

Although the local clinic is the first line of help in the community, some children may need specialist provision not only from a speech and language therapist, but from a whole team of professionals, which the local network cannot easily provide.

Maria required this kind of help, for although a full term baby she was very small, so was subsequently nursed in the Neonatal Unit. At first it was necessary to tube feed her until her weight increased sufficiently for her to be removed from the incubator; this procedure is not unusual with very small or premature babies. It was not until the tubes were removed that another problem rapidly became apparent: Maria had not developed the ability to suck. Tubes for feeding were speedily replaced and a request for help sent to the speech and language therapist.

In my experience, most parents are amazed that this expertise is within the repertoire of the therapist and not one of the medical fraternity. Of course, if you stop to think about it for a moment, the connection becomes more apparent. The movements for feeding, sucking, swallowing and then chewing, as I outlined on p. 60, precede the more complex and rapid movements needed for speech; so when difficulties occur it is the therapist, with her expert knowledge of these early skills, who is called in to solve the problem. Having a child development centre attached, the children's hospital was able to call on the therapist who, in addition to her main responsibility of caring for the children attending the centre, also provided a service for babies and children on the hospital wards.

Like other young babies who have problems with sucking and swallowing, Maria was sensitive to anything being placed in her mouth, and needed to be 'desensitised'—that is, taught to tolerate stimulation around her mouth. By gently massaging her front gums with a cotton wool bud, it was then relatively simple to encourage her to suck. This delicate movement provided enough feedback of sensation to stimulate the sucking reflex. Sadly, not all children's difficulties are solved as easily as this.

Most large cities have a child development centre, which is located within one of the major hospitals or in a children's hospital. London, however, is unusual in the range and diversity of its child development centres and no doubt the reason for this is partly historical, with different hospitals wishing to gain expertise in various areas of child development.

THE CHILD DEVELOPMENT CENTRE

You will find a wide diversity in the kinds of service provided by different child development centres; many are what is known as 'district' and others, far fewer in number, are 'regional'. Those that are district usually serve the population in the surrounding area, whereas regional centres serve a whole area of the country and usually specialise in one aspect of child development. For example, the Nuffield Centre, attached to the Royal Ear Nose and Throat Hospital in London, specialises in a particular type of speech difficulty known as 'dyspraxia': so this is probably the centre to which professionals would choose to send a child with this type of problem, for another opinion.

Whether regional or district, each centre hosts a team of highly qualified professionals, usually led by a paediatrician or neuropaediatrician. Don't let these long medical names intimidate you. A paediatrician is simply a consultant doctor who has specialist knowledge of children's health and developmental problems, whilst the neuropaediatrician has further specialist skills, to deal with a whole range of neurological problems (pertaining to the brain and nervous system). The other professionals in the team each contribute a specialist skill: other doctors, speech and language therapists, physiotherapists, occupational therapists, a clinical psychologist, an audiologist, nursery nurses, a nursery teacher, and of course all the staff who deal with administration, to ensure the smooth running of the centre.

Figure 6 summarises the different professionals with whom a therapist works at a child development centre (CDC).

A child can be referred to a child development centre at any age, should a doctor, parent or therapist be concerned about an aspect of development. Fortunately, the majority of children are referred earlier rather than later, and therapists will always act immediately if they notice anything unusual, or if they suspect any delay in development. 'Early' usually means between birth and three years. In this way, difficulties can be identified at an early stage of development and the appropriate help obtained. Some conditions such as a physical disability, for example cerebral palsy, can frequently be identified soon after birth, especially if severe, and advice on management can be given immediately. This may involve the speech and language therapist, since many conditions cause problems with feeding. Equally, many of the more obvious conditions known as syndromes, of which Down's Syndrome is the most widely known, are also recognisable soon after birth.

Children with many other conditions will be referred, who will also have speech and language difficulties. Then there are those children who have very specific and often severe difficulties with speech and language development, in fact with the whole process of communication, who may also find their way to a centre. These children are frequently very clumsy; they have poor motor co-ordination, a term which refers to their ability to move easily and sequence everyday

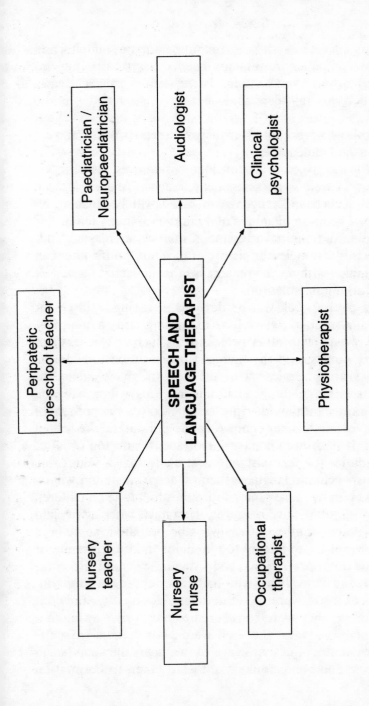

Figure 6. Who the therapist works with at the CDC.

movements such as walking, running, hopping, jumping and the finer, smaller movements needed for picking up and holding objects and writing. These deficits can be clearly identified in a full team assessment.

The Role of Speech and Language Therapists within the Child Development Team
In the majority of child development centres, which offer therapy as well as an assessment, much of the work done by the speech and language therapist will be undertaken with one or more members of a multidisciplinary team. For example, for an initial assessment, joint clinics may be held, and in this way a clearer picture of the child's difficulties can be obtained with much greater ease than if each professional was working in isolation.

Part of the week will be devoted to seeing children for individual therapy, as well as organising and running language groups with other professionals such as teachers and nursery nurses, and the therapist may well be providing a home visiting service, with the aim of giving advice to parents within the home environment. This will probably be done jointly with another professional, often the pre-school home visiting teacher (known as the peripatetic pre-school teacher). Flexibility is most important, for on top of all of these duties the therapist will most likely have a senior role in the speech and language therapy department and will be called upon by more junior colleagues to advise on children with whom they have concerns. Therapists working in child development centres must always be prepared, sometimes at short notice, to lecture to the members of their team, or to some other professional body, on an aspect of their work.

Jack and Paul, twins who had experienced feeding difficulties at birth, were monitored very closely after they left hospital, as they were considered to be 'at risk' owing to a difficult birth. Jack and Paul were poor feeders from the very beginning, but by the age of two years they had begun to refuse food and drink. They were taken to hospital on numerous occasions in a 'dehydrated state'—that is to say they did not have enough fluid for normal survival. At the same time it became apparent that they were not developing language in the normal way, for they had their own shared communication system with which they were quite happy.

By the age of three they had begun receiving help in a pre-school language group at the child development centre, and at the same time the speech and language therapist was giving advice to the parents on the question of the twins' feeding difficulties, in consultation with the clinical psychologist, since it was felt that by refusing food they were being extremely manipulative.

Jack and Paul are examples of children who, at a young age, have received the expert help of the multidisciplinary team at the child development centre, in which the speech and language therapist played a key role. Jody and Mark had totally different problems, but even so, both received help from the expert team at the child development centre.

Jody's mum noticed that her face had begun to get a little fatter on one side. Jody was only two years old at the time and at first her mum thought she had inadvertently collided with something, a common occurrence at this age. However, the lower left side of her face continued to swell, and in a state of high anxiety Jody's mum took her to the doctor. Greatly concerned, he referred her to the children's hospital, where a non-cancerous growth was diagnosed. Because of its location, in a sensitive area of her face, it was only partially removed and Jody was referred to the child development centre for therapy and the advice her parents needed on how to manage the problem. Jody required a great deal of help and support from the speech and language therapist for both feeding and speech, which were severely affected. She was given a whole range of sucking, blowing, and tongue and lip exercises; also, ice was used to increase the sensitivity inside her mouth, to help her put her tongue in the right place for feeding and for speech sounds. Even though Jody has now entered a special school, her progress is still monitored at the child development centre, because of the recurrence of the growth and therefore the need for therapy. Parts of the growth are removed from time to time but sadly, because it is invasive, in other words it has affected many parts of Jody's face, it is not easy totally to remove it by surgery.

Mark, a bouncy four-year-old, had problems of another kind. Although he had delayed language development, it appeared that whenever he was put in a situation he found threatening, he adopted the personality of one of his favourite characters—Thomas the tank engine, the fat controller, Scotty, and so on. Mark's mother found this situation both puzzling and confusing, as she was never sure how to address each new character or, indeed, how to deal with the whole situation. Mark was assessed by the paediatrician, who asked both the speech and language therapist and the clinical psychologist to see him.

Together, the therapist and clinical psychologist set up activities in a language group, which helped his language development yet at the same time were unthreatening. Even so, at first Mark continued to switch from character to character, only gradually becoming more amenable to persuasion, so that the therapist was increasingly able to encourage him to be 'himself'. Everyone working with Mark felt that his somewhat bizarre behaviour was his way of coping with poor language, for as his language improved, the behaviour disappeared. The benefits of the expertise available at the child development centre are very apparent for a child like Mark, whose difficulties were far from straightforward. Increasingly, however, professionals in the Health Service are attempting to bring help to where their patients live, rather than the other way round.

THE LOCAL NETWORK

Somewhat like the public school or City old boy network, you will also find, at local level, an extremely effective professional network which you can make use of to help you with your child's problems. Close working relationships are built up between doctors, nurses, health visitors, therapists, educational psychologists—in fact just about any professional working within the community. 'Networking', as it is called these days, crosses all professional and institutional divides. It makes little difference whether we work for health, education, social services, mental health or any other employing organisation: we make contact across these divisions to provide a complete framework to assess and solve children's problems. Good communication is undoubtedly the basic ingredient for this kind of teamwork to be successful.

When a child who is referred for speech and language therapy reveals other puzzling problems, the therapist will naturally want to know more. Referral to various consultants can be most helpful; perhaps the child has hearing problems, or recurring infections of throat, ears, and chest, and maybe these infections are the cause of the hearing loss. A referral to the ear, nose and throat consultant may go a long way to solve a speech and language problem, if the hearing difficulties can be resolved.

The key workers in the local network team, however, are really the clinical medical officers (CMOs). They provide a service to both pre-school and school age children. When an unusual problem arises, it is usually from them that the therapist will first seek advice, since they are trained to assess the overall development of pre-school children over whom concern has been expressed.

When a therapist suspects a child has developmental problems as well as poor speech and language, she first approaches the parents to discuss her concerns, before embarking on a referral to anyone else. It is not an easy task to suggest to parents that their child may have other problems, since they are already so anxious about the more obvious poor speech and language. Yet, in the best interests of everyone, especially the child, it is essential to have as much information as possible, so that accurate decisions about the usefulness of therapy can be made. If a child's general development is delayed and his speech and language are delayed to the same degree, then it is unfair to expect him to make accelerated progress with the help of therapy. It places unrealistic pressure on a child and would be most unwise, possibly doing more harm than good. So you can see how the assessment by the clinical medical officer can be crucial for the therapist.

CMOs use a variety of check-lists to chart a child's development, but the two most commonly used are the Stycar Sequences, by Mary Sheridan, and the Griffiths Developmental Scales; both provide a description of the normal development of basic skills. With the Stycar Sequences, four broad developmental areas are covered from birth to five years—posture and gross movements, vision and fine movements, hearing and speech, social behaviour and play. The Griffiths Scales were introduced in the 1950s, designed purely for babies up to the age of two years, but this range was extended in 1970 to include children up to the age of eight. Six areas of development are assessed—movements such as crawling, rolling, standing, walking, running; personal and social; hearing and speech; eye and hand co-ordination; performance tests; and practical reasoning. Each section has a score and the differences between these can give the therapist a good idea whether a child's problem is specific, or just part of a more general developmental delay.

As I mentioned on p. 64, many children with speech and language difficulties are also poorly co-ordinated. Sometimes, before little Joe opens his mouth, we know the kind of speech and language problems he may have: it is the way he lurches through the door of the therapy room, narrowly missing every obstacle in his path, continually tripping over his own feet, that indicates something is wrong. Zac was just like this. He had a really severe speech problem; he also fell over frequently, and walked in a very odd way for a three-and-a-half year-old, with his legs wide apart, reminiscent of a fifteen-month-old toddler who has just started to walk. Once underway, he leaned forward at an alarming angle, appearing constantly to be on the point of tipping over.

Zac was referred to a consultant neuropaediatrician, and from her assessment he was able to receive help at his local nursery from both the physiotherapist and the occupational therapist, specialists in working with children. They are known as the paediatric physiotherapist and paediatric occupational therapist; the term paediatric means that they work with children.

Zac needed help to improve all his movements, whether they were for walking, picking things up or for talking, so at first the speech and language therapist concentrated on helping him actually make the general movements required for speech—what we call 'lip and tongue exercises', a sort of oral physiotherapy. Unless you can, for example, raise the tip of your tongue, you are not likely to be able to make all those speech sounds which require that movement.

Next Zac was taught how to make more specific speech sounds and how to move easily from one to another, but this is not as simple as it sounds. In order to remember the sounds, young children must have a visual symbol, something which gives them as much information about that sound as possible. They are far too young to understand traditional letters, so we use either representational pictures—for example a candle for a 'p' or a dripping tap for a 't'. An increasing number of therapists, however, are now using a symbol system called 'Letterland', in which the traditional letters of the alphabet become a real person—for example, 't' is Ticking Tom the Telecom man and you can hear the quiet ticking sound he makes as you listen to his telephone. The wonderful stories of the characters, the alliterative nature of their names and the cartoon-like drawings of them provide a powerful mnemonic. A mnemonic is any kind of aid that will help you remember facts; most of us have our own favourite—for example, I can never recall how to spell 'receive', so without fail I recite to myself, ' "i" before "e" except after "c"!'

Zac loved Letterland from the start, but needed some extra visual reminders for the vowels, which are not as easily seen when they are articulated as the majority of the consonant sounds. He was taught some finger 'cues', special finger signs produced close to the mouth, each cue representing a different vowel sound; here the occupational therapist's help was sought, since Zac didn't move his fingers very well either!

It quickly became apparent that Zac did not understand how sounds are organised in words, so he was taught about the particular features of speech sounds—whether they are noisy or quiet, short or long, explosive or hissy; that there are consonant sounds at the beginning, middle and ends of words, plus other rules which you and I learn without realising we are learning them.

Understandably, Zac's language was rather delayed as a result of his speech difficulties, but in a group he soon moved from single word utterances to two, three and more words in a sentence. With close co-operation between all the therapists, nursery school and parents, Zac made excellent progress in all the areas of his development, particularly his speech.

The Educational Psychologist
Concern over a child's general learning can be a reason for the speech and language therapist to refer the child to a particular colleague in the local network: the educational psychologist. From my own experience, there is some confusion over the role of the educational psychologist. Psychologists and psychiatrists are frequently presumed to be one and the same, which is inaccurate. Psychiatrists deal with individuals who are mentally ill, whereas psychologists study people's minds and how they work. An educational psychologist therefore has the skills to understand and advise on children's needs in relation to their social development, their learning and schooling. Although the majority of their work is with children of school age, educational psychologists also

work with pre-school children. There are times when the developmental profile we receive from the clinical medical officers is insufficient and we would like more information on the child. Through their observations and assessment, psychologists are able to give an indication of general learning ability, and in particular a child's learning strengths and weaknesses.

Martin was a child about whom we could easily have been mistaken, had it not been for the help of the educational psychologist. His speech and language skills were really poor, and so was his co-ordination, but from our observations he also appeared to have delays in other areas of his development. An amiable, unconcerned little boy, he just appeared to be rather slow all round. We did, however, have a degree of concern about our observations because of Martin's sister. An older child, she behaved like a second mother—not the encouraging kind, more the smothering kind. Poor Martin was totally dominated by this articulate and well-intentioned little girl; he only had to grunt and his desires were instantly gratified.

When seen by the educational psychologist, Martin was found to have skills quite appropriate for his age in areas where language was not needed; his problem was more to do with motivation. Why bother when learning anything was such an effort? Far easier to relax and let someone else do it for you. Without these valuable insights it could have been easy to perceive Martin as a rather slow child and not provide him with the most appropriate management which, naturally, included changing the behaviour of his sister. When it was explained to her how she could help him to speak, by making him ask for things rather than pointing, life immediately changed for Martin. He was also encouraged to request verbally in the language therapy group he attended, and with the concerted approach from home and the therapist, within nine months he no longer required our help.

THE PORTAGE PROJECT

Parents of children with special needs have the opportunity to participate in what is known as the 'Portage Project'. Briefly, Portage is a home visiting educational service for pre-school children with special needs. Parents become 'teachers' under the guidance of a trained Portage home visitor.

Portage, a town in Wisconsin, USA, was where the idea for the service evolved and the first project was piloted. Portage looks at all areas of a child's development, finds out what the child can do and uses this to help him learn. The emphasis is always on the positive, building on what the child can do. Children from zero to five years can be helped, by parents and professionals working in partnership. The key worker in the Portage team is the home visitor, whose responsibility it is to visit parents and child on a weekly basis in order to discuss progress with parents and together plan the next week's activities. Figure 7 shows how it works.

The Portage Week

One of the most important skills a child will be acquiring between birth and five years is of course language: Portage has a large section on language development, which a speech and language therapist will actually teach to home visitors on their training programme. If a child has a communication problem it is highly likely that a therapist will already be involved, advising on management, but she will continuously maintain contact with the home visitor to make the most effective use of everyone's skills and time.

Portage home visitors come from a wide range of backgrounds, but all are specially trained in Portage methods. Some are professionals who have been allocated time from their jobs to visit one family, while others are volunteers with a great deal of experience of working with young children. Occasionally, speech and language therapists are given 'time' from their work to visit a family, but this is rare,

Figure 7.

*Home Visitor
visits weekly*

*A goal is selected:
a small step,
aiming for
success by
the end of
the week*

The Portage Week

*How to teach this goal
is discussed, then tried
out by both home visitor
and parent*

*Parents practise
activity daily
with their
child,
recording
progress on
Activity Chart*

*Details of the
agreed activity
are written on
an 'Activity Chart'*

Chart reproduced by courtesy of West Sussex Portage Services mainly because of the difficulties of negotiating who pays for their time and deciding who will do the therapist's job whilst she is working on Portage.

Supervision for the team of home visitors is provided by a part-time educational psychologist, and a full-time teacher will have overall responsibility for the co-ordination of the team. Representatives from education, health, social services and the voluntary agencies form an advisory team with a parent, and in this way the Portage team can maintain close contacts with these organisations. One of the great strengths of Portage, which parents, teachers and therapists will immediately recognise, is the successful relationship that exists between parents and professionals working in harmony for the benefit of the child.

PRE-SCHOOL PLACEMENTS

Throughout the country, pre-school education is available to parents in a variety of forms. There are, for example, both state-funded and private nursery education, playgroups and day care facilities. However, as many parents are aware, in Britain, the quality and availability of pre-school education depends largely on where you live. Thankfully, irrespective of patchy provision, there is a positive side to all this: a certain number of places are always set aside in state nurseries for children with special needs. The Pre-School Playgroups Association also organises special opportunities groups in most areas. Certainly, those children with whom we deal as speech and language therapists benefit enormously from the contact with other children. This is not to detract from the vast amount of chatter that takes place in the home, but sooner or later we have to learn to live with other people outside the family, for as humans we are essentially social beings. Also, the language of the nursery or playgroup is rather different from that of home. Expectations are different and it is a new learning situation.

State-Funded Nurseries

Mention state nurseries these days and most people will throw up their arms in despair and declare that there are all too few available. However, it is important to remember that they do accept a certain number of children with special needs. How many will really depend on the size of the nursery, since it is important to have a large enough number of other children in order to provide the right kind of stimulation for those with special needs.

How do speech and language therapy departments provide a service to those children who are attending nurseries? As always, much depends on what the local community needs. Some Health Authorities, for example, may have ten or more nurseries within their boundaries, as in some areas of large cities like London, whereas others may only have one or two. Where there is a large number of nurseries, it makes sense to have one, or even several therapists, with one of them acting as the co-ordinator of a small team, whose sole responsibility it is to see the children. However, a therapist with only a few nurseries to visit would devote less time to them and work in a slightly different way from colleagues who were responsible for a larger number. Therapists who enjoy a peripatetic life will most certainly find this kind of work demanding and at times exhausting, for one day their work may be carried out in little more than a broom cupboard, whilst at other times they may have the luxury of a well-equipped room.

Any therapist working full time in nurseries might have a programme something like this:

— Visit every nursery at least once a week.

— Assess all the children with speech and language difficulties.

— From those assessments set up therapy programmes for the children on an individual basis or in groups. For some children both might be needed.

— Spend time talking to staff so that they are aware of the programmes and can do some follow-up work when the therapist is not at the nursery.

— Provide in-service training for nursery staff as a rolling programme—this would include subjects such as the normal development of language, speech and language difficulties, attention and listening skills, social skills, and the relevance of play to language development. It might also be necessary to provide information on special needs children and their particular problems with communication—for example those with Down's Syndrome, physical disability, learning disability and language disorder. The language of some of the children may be so limited that they will need to use a different communication system, known as an augmentative communication system, such as manual signing (using hand signs) or written symbols, and everyone working with them will have to be taught those systems.

— Work closely with parents, involving them in the therapy work and helping them to understand the nature of their child's problem. The most popular way to do this is by giving informal chats to groups of parents at the nursery—a sort of in-service for parents. Some parents prefer a more intimate chat alone and occasionally ask the therapist home for a cup of tea and a talk.

If they are not extremely diligent and well organised, professionals such as speech and language therapists, who move from place to place in the course of their work, can find themselves short of time to make those vital contacts with colleagues from other disciplines, who are also working with the children. Understandably, parents can become overwhelmed and confused by a never-ending stream of professionals asking them to do a bewildering number of tasks. Frequently, when this kind of situation arises, one of them is nominated as a 'key' worker whose responsibility is to maintain contact with parents and act as a link with all others involved with their child.

Exhausting as it sounds, a service like this can only really be provided when there are sufficient nurseries to justify it. We have to be rather more realistic when there are fewer nurseries and therefore fewer children requiring our help. Therapists are innovative people, and even though only part of their week can be devoted to nurseries, they will be making the most creative use of that time. It may be used something like this:

— By 'screening' children who are causing concern to nursery staff; screening, as I mentioned in Chapter 1 (p. 24), is a very rapid assessment procedure to establish whether or not there is a problem.

— Every child with communication difficulties is likely to be receiving help from another therapist at the local clinic or child development centre, so the visiting therapist is well placed to convey to nursery staff the details of this work and to give advice on how they can help.

— The flow of information is a two-way process, since colleagues working with the children elsewhere in the district will want to know how they are mixing with children in the nursery and, generally, how they are progressing.

— Giving talks to nursery staff and parents and being the source of information on all aspects of communication are very important parts of the work, whether it is a full- or part-time job for the therapist.

— Perhaps one of the key aspects of this way of working is acting as a co-ordinator between the nursery and the speech and language therapy service.

Therapists may find themselves in the uncomfortable position of having to see far more children than had originally been anticipated—in my experience a situation that is not unusual. One therapist recently described her experiences in attempting to deal with an overwhelming number of referrals within nurseries, all requiring her help. How, she wondered, could she solve the problem when no more funding for extra time was available? Wisely, she took her dilemma to the staff in the nurseries where she worked. What, she asked, did they think would be the best way for her to use her valuable time?

She had anticipated replies suggesting she spend her time only with those children with severe communication difficulties. Instead, to her surprise, the staff requested more in-service training. They argued that, if they could increase their own knowledge, they could then make a substantial contribution to the progress of children with speech and language problems. This would then free the therapist to work with those children whose needs were greatest and, with her advice and guidance, they could assume responsibility for the rest. Once again, the answer to a problem had been provided by good communication.

When money is in short supply it may not be possible to provide anything as innovative as I have described, and the best that can be done is to have a kind of 'hot line' service. One therapist is given the responsibility to look into requests for help, or to give talks. Thankfully, there are always ways and means of dealing with what at first may appear to be intractable problems for the Health Trust struggling to cope with ever-increasing demands on its purse.

Nowadays, most people who work with special needs children acknowledge the sense of giving help as early as possible, but very reasonably ask the question, 'Who pays?' Frequently, the solution has been found through co-operation between Health and Education and currently, across the country, many speech and language therapy posts for nurseries are joint-funded. In this way the desperate needs of many of the children have been met.

The long-term future of these arrangements is, however, a cause for concern. At the moment, agreements are made between the Local Education Authority (LEA), who provides the funds for special needs children, and a Health Trust, but with an increasing number of schools opting out of local education control, we must ask ourselves who in the future will be responsible for the children, particularly if the role of the LEA is reduced or even becomes redundant.

Playgroups
Playgroups are a prolific and valuable provider of facilities for pre-school children. Unlike state-funded nurseries they are run by parents who may not be teachers. Instead there is a recognised training programme for registered playgroup workers, which is undertaken by many playgroup leaders. Speech and language therapists contribute to this training, as well as giving talks on a regular basis to local groups of playgroup leaders. It is not unusual for children with special needs to attend playgroups, and in these circumstances the therapist will talk to the playgroup leader, usually by 'phone and follow-up correspondence, to explain the child's problems and what is being done about them. Time permitting, a visit to the playgroup might be arranged, particularly where the staff are experiencing problems with the management of the child.

Assessment Nurseries and Centres
There are children whose difficulties are so puzzling or complex that they require far more specialist help than can be provided at any of the more regular pre-school facilities I have so far discussed. Understandably, many parents may be perplexed by the number of pre-school facilities which are available for their children. What, then, is different about assessment nurseries and centres? It is quite simply this: here, under one roof, they will find a team of professionals who between them represent a pool of expertise dedicated to the specific needs of these children. During the child's stay, which may be weeks or years, he will be assessed and a diagnosis made; meanwhile he will be receiving the kind

of therapy and teaching unavailable to him elsewhere. Many authorities make special provision for these children, but because of the range of staff needed, it is supported by both the Education and Health Authorities. When so many individuals from diverse backgrounds find themselves together every day, good humour, tolerance and a clear understanding of the work of other professionals are essential for successful teamwork. Figure 8 shows the number of people from Health and Education who work at the centre.

Whilst most professionals would agree that the apparently never-ending meetings eat into valuable therapy time, in special centres like these regular team meetings are essential for the exchange of information, and are also an opportunity to build relationships with other staff. The head of the centre is responsible for the overall co-ordination of the team, as well as day-to-day organisation. The team speech and language therapist may attend the centre for only part of the week, or may be there on a full-time basis, but in either case her duties would be the same:

- To assess the children, sometimes jointly with other staff.
- To meet the parents in order to discuss their child's progress and therapy work.
- To work with children on therapy programmes either individually or in groups.
- To work with the children and another member of staff, for example, the physiotherapist or teacher.
- To communicate with outside agencies like social services.
- To provide in-service training for other staff at regular intervals.
- To discuss therapy work with staff at the local nurseries, where children from the centre also attend, so that they can help as much as possible.

The children need opportunities to mix with able children of their own age, so some of them will only attend the centre on a part-time basis and will spend the rest of the week attending a local nursery or playgroup. This enables all the

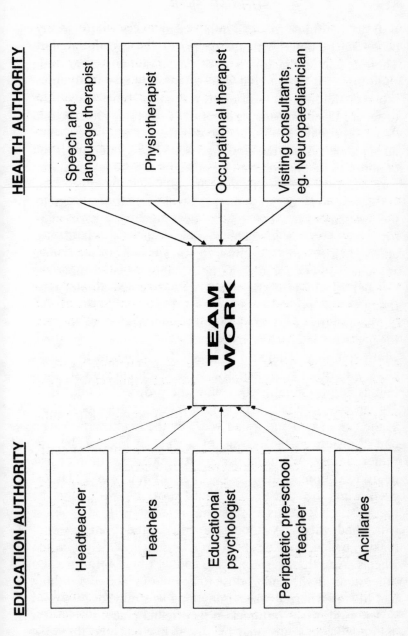

HEALTH AUTHORITY

- Speech and language therapist
- Physiotherapist
- Occupational therapist
- Visiting consultants, eg. Neuropaediatrician

TEAM WORK

EDUCATION AUTHORITY

- Headteacher
- Teachers
- Educational psychologist
- Peripatetic pre-school teacher
- Ancillaries

Figure 8. Team work in a pre-school assessment centre.

staff to see how the children manage elsewhere and to become acquainted with every aspect of their development. There is one key factor to all of this: a non-communicating child may not be stimulated to speak if he is placed with a group of children who, for whatever reason, have an inability to speak. Place him amongst normally speaking children and you will probably, in time, discover the extent of the speech and language he understands and uses. I have been surprised on more than one occasion by just how much these children can say in the right environment.

Because they are so young, the children may only attend the assessment nursery, or the local nursery or playgroup, for a few days a week. This flexible pattern of attendance, although ideal for the children, inevitably causes a huge amount of work for the therapist, since it can double the number of children she needs to see in one week, even though she is possibly not there on a full-time basis. To see all the children who need help is sometimes rather like the juggler who keeps five balls in the air at the same time, whilst spinning a plate on his nose! To show how therapists work with other staff, and how vital communication is when time is at a premium, let's follow the progress of one child.

John was originally referred for therapy to the local clinic at the age of two-and-a-half years by the health visitor who had also noticed that, even for a child of his age, he was rather clumsy. When he was a little older, his mother was heard to comment that he was likely to 'fall over a feather, even when he'd seen it'. Whilst working with him the therapist noticed his obsessional interest with any object which had wheels. As soon as he entered the room he would make a collection, line them up and then endlessly spin the wheels. And that wasn't all. He couldn't bear furniture and other items in the doll's house to be out of place. Everything had to stay where it was. If anything was moved, he would shriek until it was put back in its original place.

Puzzled and concerned by this behaviour, the therapist asked the clinical medical officer to see John, as well as a more senior therapist in the department. It was agreed by everyone that John should be referred to the assessment centre following a visit from the pre-school peripatetic teacher. These are knowledgeable and flexible people who have not only superb specialised teaching skills, but also the ability to be astute, diplomatic, yet firm. In the field of special education, everyone will agree, they are a rarity.

John was considered a most suitable candidate for the centre and entered after a short wait. Here he was placed with children of his own age and within a few days, once he had become familiar with the staff, the long process of a multi-disciplinary assessment began. John was observed over a period of three months and during this time a full picture emerged of his language, learning, social skills and behaviour.

The longer the speech and language therapist worked with him and observed his behaviour, the more convinced she became that his difficulties in understanding and using language were not his primary problem. More important was his difficulty in understanding and interpreting the world and people in it. Other staff agreed with this. John's profile resembled that of a child who has autism. For a diagnosis, the opinion of a medical consultant who was a specialist in autism was essential, and so arrangements were made for her to see John. Her views agreed with those of the staff: John was indeed autistic.

It was decided that it would be in John's best interests to remain at the assessment centre, where it was possible for him to have an intensive teaching and communication therapy programme. At the same time, for part of the week he attended a local nursery, where the therapist spent some time talking to the staff, advising them on the best way to help John to communicate. At this stage it was important for John to learn to make eye contact, to look at objects or people he wanted to acknowledge, to learn to point, and to be persuaded to play with toys other than cars. He also needed to be taught that words have different functions—

for example, some are for labelling, others for actions and so on. As John progressed and learned these skills, the therapist was then able to advise the nursery staff on the next stage of therapy.

Locations of assessment centres vary enormously from area to area: sometimes they are attached to a school, sometimes a hospital. On occasion, because they have been developed through the initiative of a particular individual, they are not attached to any institution.

So far we have only thought about state-funded assessment centres, but there are alternatives which have been established often by concerned individuals or charities for one group of children with a particular disability, for example Down's Syndrome. Parents appreciate choice and the opportunity to take their child to a centre which appears to have a great deal of expertise directed towards children like their own.

In recognition of their substantial needs, some Health and Education Authorities have organised nursery classes for children with specific language disorder. Everyone who understands their disability is aware that these children are likely to have long-term difficulty in learning language, even though in every other way they appear to learn in the normal fashion. Intensive specialist teaching and therapy begin at an age when a child would ordinarily attend a nursery and are not left until children reach school age. Of course, speech therapists have always made special provision for these children; but as far back as I can recall our concern has been that this is not enough. With this particular disability, as with any other, intensive work is essential from an early age.

Ideally, services would be planned to give the children the widest range of experience combined with intensive therapy and teaching. Regretfully, we must accept that we do not live in an ideal world, so the next best move is to be aware of what is available if your child has a disability. As the nation has become better educated and, through consumer programmes, aware that people can formulate a powerful

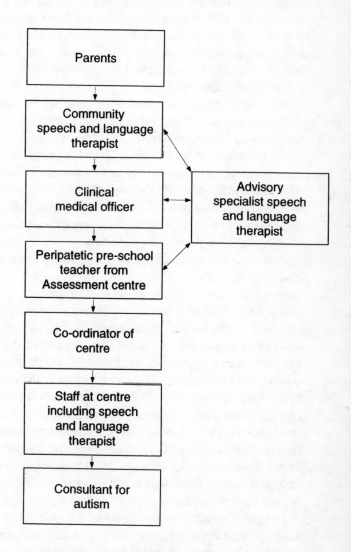

Figure 9. Showing how John's assessment progressed.

voice to influence government policy, more parents are
making use of the public platform of radio and television to
secure a better world for their children. Professionals, on
the other hand, cannot for ethical reasons speak out to support this or that cause, even though they may be aware of
serious shortcomings.

Recently I heard of one imaginative scheme to help children in a socially deprived area. For some parents, who had
a variety of social, emotional and financial problems, getting
their children to the speech and language therapist, the
health visitor, even to the doctor, was a major undertaking.
The aim of the 'pre-school project', as it came to be known,
was to support parents' interest in their children's early
development and to provide learning opportunities for pre-
school children within the community.

Several areas of a child's development were seen as absolutely vital if the children were to make the most of their
school life. Amongst these, lack of language, together with
social and emotional skills, would most certainly prevent the
children from making the most of the opportunities offered
in nursery and primary school. To assist with the pre-school
project, home visitors were trained by a therapist and an
educational psychologist in early language development and
play. As the project was a pilot scheme, really a piece of
research, not every family in the area could be visited. Using
records, certain families with children aged between
eighteen months and two-and-a-half years were selected
and asked for their consent. Most agreed, welcoming any
help that came their way so long as it was not going to be
'nosey or interfering'.

In order to measure progress, a group of children was
selected as 'control group'. In research terms, this involves
matching as clearly as possible the children in the group who
are receiving help with those who are in the control group
and not receiving help—by, for example, age, sex, location
and housing condition. The outcome of all this extra help
was assessed when the children entered nursery school,

where it was found that they were better language users and did not need further therapy. The project was seen as a useful and essential piece of research, by helping children early in their life.

Understandably, parents are increasingly unwilling to put a child with speech, language or communication impairment into any kind of pre-school provision unless there is some assurance of expert help. Thank goodness, the majority of children do not require the intensive therapy provided by specialist nurseries and centres. However, they also have needs which cannot be ignored and I hope I have shown how, as therapists, we are using our skills in the most effective and innovative way to meet the very special needs of all pre-school children who have communication difficulties.

4 Language Disorder

It is not uncommon for those who do not understand the complexities of our bewildering world of language to label all children who cannot communicate as stupid or mentally backward. No doubt at some time or another we have all been guilty of thinking it. Even among fellow professionals there remains a degree of ignorance, something I find puzzling in today's well-informed society. Now and then, for various reasons, a child still 'slips through the net' and his language problems remain unidentified. Chris is one such child, although if you met him now you would consider him just a normal 18-year-old who needs extra teaching help for his 'A' levels. Life, however, was not always so kind to him.

When he started school at the age of four-and-a-half, Chris had great difficulty understanding language and stringing words together in a way that made any kind of sense. It took a long time, but eventually he was identified as a child with specific language disorder. His mother, Pat, remembers that he was unlike any of her other seven children: 'I knew he was not mentally backward, but I also knew there was something very different about him that was wrong. I just didn't know what it was.'

Chris could do many things which convinced Pat he was intelligent, even though his understanding was poor and he used very little language. He was a very practical child: for example, at the age of two-and-a-half he was building Lego models; at three-and-a-half he repaired a toy train using a screwdriver and accurately replaced the dead batteries.

Her story of attempting to find out what was wrong with

Chris would be an unusual occurrence today, but 14 years ago things were a little different. When she raised her concerns with her doctor and later with a consultant, she was given a patronising 'pat on the head' and told not to worry because he was just 'a slow talker and a late developer'.

School became an increasingly hostile place for Chris; failure was part of his daily existence. He did not understand what was going on and sadly was labelled as mentally backward. He was further humiliated by being made to stand in front of the class for not following instructions. 'Cannot understand' was interpreted by a somewhat unsympathetic and no doubt harassed teacher as 'doesn't want to and is being difficult'. Understandably, his behaviour deteriorated. Frustration turned into aggression and fights.

It was an educational psychologist who came to Chris's assistance. Puzzled by the boy's difficulties in understanding and using language, he found him to have well above average intelligence in tasks which did not rely on language. With added help from a speech therapist experienced in dealing with children like Chris, his problems were finally identified and, within a few months, he was in a language unit, a small class in mainstream school with specialised therapy and teaching facilities.

Very quickly Chris started to learn to read and through this was taught to understand spoken language with the support of a simple signing system. In time he improved and moved to a small class in the mainstream of the same school, eventually transferring to a comprehensive school sympathetic to children with various kinds of learning difficulties. Since then he has successfully gained six GCSEs and is studying hard to go to university.

Every profession, including speech and language therapy, has its own sort of language—a type of shorthand by which individuals communicate with each other. To the lay person it is near-meaningless, with words and phrases that could easily come from another language. Do not be put off if you hear any of the following: specific language disorder, language disorder, aphasia, dysphasia, dyspraxia, specific developmental language disorder; they are terms which are used to describe the complex sort of language problems experienced by children such as Chris. A few years ago a study was undertaken on language units, and something like thirty terms were used to describe the children's communication difficulties, so it is possible you may hear even more than those I have listed!

I have already mentioned that as many as one in seven school age children are estimated to have some kind of speech and language problem, from a simple lisp to the sort of complex language difficulties experienced by Chris; of these, it is thought that approximately one in 1,000 have specific language disorder. In the various studies undertaken to assess the size of the problem, which I outlined on p. 43, not everyone agreed on what was meant by the terms 'mild', 'moderate' and 'severe', so perhaps we need to view the figure of one in 1,000 with a degree of suspicion. For those of us actively engaged in the field of language disorder, experience would suggest that this is an underestimate, and there are more children out there with this particular problem than we have previously been led to believe.

You may well be wondering at this point what it is about these children that makes them different from the others who have speech and language problems. What is special and different about language disorder? What distinguishes the Christophers of this world from other children who apparently have similar disabilities?

Firstly, and this may come as a surprise to some people, the problems are not caused by such things as hearing loss, emotional problems or learning difficulties. There appears to be no obvious reason why the child is not learning language in the normal way. Secondly, despite a great deal of help, usually from an early age, from speech and language therapists, the children make little progress and the problems remain alarmingly severe. Finally, they have not learned their own language following the usual route.

It is vitally important that you listen to your child. If he has no difficulties, you will know how smooth his progression is along the road of learning to speak. He goes from one stage to the other with amazing ease; it is a predictable route. However, things are completely different with children who have language disorder. For them, it is rather like British Rail on a bad day. These children go on a somewhat different route to get to their destination, stopping at many of the wrong places along the way and arriving—assuming they do arrive—a great deal later than planned.

I have known children like Chris who have no meaningful understanding of their own language, a disability so severe they cannot even recognise their own name. Other children with different, but just as complex, problems, have so few speech sounds in their language that all they are capable of saying is a few vowels, or just one or two words, to express their thoughts and feelings.

Some of these children may have learned some of the right things at the wrong time. Take, for example, some of the words and ideas learned at the age of two years: many of these may be learned at four years. It is of course quite possible that at the same time they may have learned other language in a fragmented sort of way. Often, what many children have learned is applied in the wrong way, according to their own set of rules.

Let us look at Chris again. At six-and-a-half he had huge gaps in his understanding of language. He understood some apparently more complex language, but other language far simpler, which should have been learned at three years, was missing. He had no idea of the words relating to time and space; no conception of inferences or implied nuances of language. Jokes, however simple, and colloquial language like, 'you're driving me round the bend', 'hit the nail on the head', were meaningless. At times, Chris even misinterpreted the everyday 'ums, ers, ha-has' we use all the time. It is hardly surprising that his world, when it came to language, was one of utter confusion.

Stop and think about it. There are few tasks we can ask children to do without using language. Even the simplest of things, such as getting dressed, require an explanation. 'Your socks are in your top drawer, your pants in the airing cupboard and your shirt on the chair. Now go and get dressed.' You can hear yourself saying it, can't you? Chris and others like him, strange though it may seem, just cannot understand that amount of language. Words such as 'in', 'top' and 'on' have no meaning for them.

You will recall that children with language disorder often show their intelligence in other ways. Chris, for example, at the age of four, was able to recall a visit to Windsor Safari Park two years previously. On the second visit he was able to tell his astounded parents, in his own limited way, how to get there. He remembered everything in detail, the places he wanted to go and the animals he wanted to see, even though at the age of two he had had no useful understanding of language.

TYPES OF LANGUAGE DISORDER

Difficulties with Understanding Language

For the sake of simplicity, problems experienced by children with language disorder can be described as falling into three broad areas. There are those who, like Chris, have difficulty understanding language, but not all the children have exactly his kind of problem. Some may understand nothing, whilst others, less severely impaired, may not understand the difference between words that describe objects and words that describe actions. As far as these children are concerned, one word could quite easily be used instead of another. Then there are those who have little idea about the rules of grammar. They may not understand that, by changing the order of the words in a sentence, the meaning will also change. It's fairly obvious to you and me that there's a world of difference between 'the dog bit the man' and 'the man bit the dog'. But not to these children.

As such children progress, it becomes apparent that they do not always understand other aspects of language, like colloquialisms, irony, sarcasm and jokes, which are either interpreted in a literal fashion or are misinterpreted. Sometimes even simple, basic associations such as 'bat and ball' are misunderstood. When asked to draw five balls and three bats, ten-year-old Dan conscientiously did so. There was only one problem: his bats were of the spooky kind that are alive and hang upside down!

Misperceptions of words can also cause misunderstandings, a phenomenon probably experienced by some of us when learning the 'Lord's Prayer'. I well recall that for a long time I thought it was 'and we forgive them that trees pass against us'—a single incident in my life, but for children with language disorder it can happen frequently. John related this story to his teacher. He was amazed to discover that David did not understand why there were piles of earth all over the lawn. 'I told David that these were caused by modes,' he said. His teacher, trying to be helpful, suggested he meant moles. 'No,' the answer came back immediately, 'no, no, not moles, Mrs Law, modes.'

Now I am quite sure that, at some time or other, we have all met adults with problems of this kind—those for whom a touch of sarcasm is totally incomprehensible, or who never seem to see the joke, whilst the rest of us are quite literally falling apart with laughter. Reflecting on Sheridan's delightful character, Mrs Malaprop, one wonders if perhaps at some time in her life she had also suffered from a language disorder.

Occasionally it can happen that children fail to interpret other aspects of language, such as the pauses between words, rhythm, intonation and stress. In the words of the song, 'it ain't what you say, it's the way that you say it.' How we say things can and does change meaning. It can change it in many ways, and failure to understand can lead to embarrassing situations. For example, we often say one thing in such a way that it means exactly the opposite. Take, for instance, 'that's great': it can also mean 'that's awful'. Alternatively, if we put the stress on different parts of the sentence, that too can change the meaning. For instance, 'John gave an apple to Sam and then he gave an orange to Martha' can have two entirely different meanings, depending on whether or not you stress 'he'. So you see, it is not difficult to understand how children who have this kind of disability could easily get themselves into trouble, particularly in the playground, where an inoffensive remark could be misinterpreted. As a result of their inappropriate reactions to situations such as this, these children are frequently labelled as insensitive, difficult or even badly behaved.

Difficulties with Expressive Language

What may appear simple for many of us could be a real problem for some children. Take the apparently straightforward matter of learning words and putting them into sentences. There are children who have great difficulty doing this. Some of you may have heard the term 'expressive language' to describe this aspect of language. As their language develops, you may recall that children go through the stage of using one word to describe a whole host of things. Usually in their second year, extending halfway into their third year, they might, for example, use the word 'dog' to mean all four-legged animals. Many children with language disorder may not progress beyond this stage, and this means they will have a very limited vocabulary at the age of five or thereabouts, just when they are due to go to school.

Very often, children with this type of difficulty also find it hard to learn the rules that govern how words fit together in phrases and sentences. A teacher, on hearing one child say, 'Me that you give,' described his language as 'verbal salad'—a very apt description. His language had developed but he had no idea of word order, of what words went together, which came first or which came last.

As these children progress, different parts of language within a sentence are not always understood or used appropriately. Words like 'he', 'her', 'she', 'him' (personal pronouns), which refer to people, can provide exceptional difficulties. You might recall these from your own schooldays. Steve had only one personal pronoun, 'him', which he used with great frequency as a substitute for all the rest. So, for example, 'she looked at his picture' became, 'him looked at him picture'. One poor teacher became totally confused when James proudly presented his sister on her first day at school, saying, 'Mrs Earl, he is her sister and his name is Emma.'

Difficulties do not stop at the number of words a child may have learned, or the way in which he combines them to make coherent sentences. Some children have no idea how to make best use of the language they have managed to learn. They find taking turns and maintaining the topic of conversations quite beyond them, and they appear not to have learned the 'rules' or 'conventions' of conversation. They interrupt at the wrong time, ignore questions, and frustrate all attempts by others to join in the conversation. Many appear amazingly insensitive to what other people might want to say and are completely unable to engage in co-operative discussions.

Often, with great enthusiasm, they come into the conversation assuming you know everything or, more often, nothing. Politicians demonstrate similar behaviour, particularly when they are being interviewed; however, in their case it is a deliberate ploy. I recall entering a classroom one day, first thing in the morning, when Lee said to me, 'She's in there.' As you can imagine, I had absolutely no idea who Lee was referring to or, for that matter, where 'she' was, and was rather taken aback, since I had been expecting the usual cheery 'Good morning!'

Difficulties with Pronunciation
Finally, there are those children who have great difficulty with pronunciation: some find it impossible to make and sequence the rapid lip, tongue and palatal movements

necessary for articulate speech. This can extend to the muscles of the throat and larynx (voice box), and affects speech in such a way that voice is not always produced at the right moment and speech is frequently lacking in normal intonations. It takes a great deal of muscular control as well as co-ordination to start and stop your voice when you want, and at the same time make it go up and down in pitch.

Most people are unaware that, to make just one simple speech sound, an incredibly complex sequence of movements is required. When you make the explosive sound 'd', for instance, which is correctly termed a 'plosive', your tongue must move in the right direction, at the right speed, towards the right spot in your mouth with which it makes contact (in this case it's the gum ridge behind your top teeth known as the 'alveolar ridge'). Whilst doing this, it must maintain the right shape, make the right amount of surface contact and maintain the right pressure. Since it is a voiced sound, at the same time voice must be initiated at just the right moment, maintained for the right amount of time and at the right pitch. All of which goes to demonstrate how difficult it is to make just one sound!

Children's speech sounds may be so limited that some five-year-olds may only have learned one vowel sound which constitutes their total language. Mike, for example, could only say 'u' as in 'cup', but with great effect he combined it with normal rhythms and intonations, lots of gesture and facial expression and more or less made himself understood. Sam, on the other hand, had a full range of vowel sounds but not one consonant sound. Kate could only manage 'ku', so when asked to count she would say, 'ku ku ku ku ku'— one, two, three, four, five.

Associated Difficulties
You may also have noticed that your child has difficulties other than a communication disability, and wondered whether they are associated in any way. One mother once said to me of her young daughter with language disorder,

'She trips over, walks into and drops everything. She'd fall over a blade of grass in the middle of a field.' Sounds familiar? It is well documented that children with language disorder are frequently clumsy; not only do they have poor co-ordination, but they also find organising their movements, sometimes to do even the simplest task, incredibly problematical.

What do I mean by this? All of us, confronted with the task of going through a hoop without touching the sides, would do it with great ease. I have observed children with language disorder attempting the same activity and having no idea which part of their body should go first, apparently having no plan on how it should be done. Invariably they and the hoop finish up in a tangled heap on the floor.

Some children have poor memories, especially when it comes to something that has just recently occurred. Others have poor listening and attention skills, and perhaps this is predictable when language has so far been a fairly useless tool in their short lives. From their point of view, why bother, when you don't understand most of what is being said around you, or you can't respond very well and even when you do, the world appears to have no idea what you are saying.

'Why does my child have language disorder?' I have lost count of the number of times in my career distraught parents have asked me this question. No matter how many years a therapist may have been practising, when faced with this, we wish we had a succinct answer. But we have to be honest and admit that we don't always know. With other speech and language problems, such as those associated with cerebral palsy, for example, the answer is far simpler. It is obvious. The child is physically disabled and his speech and language impairment is associated with this. This is not the case with language disorder.

Never be afraid to ask. As parents you must feel free to discuss your child's problems in the fullest way, for even if there is no tidy answer, you rightly require information.

Above all, do not blame yourselves. You will already have gone through agonies of soul-searching, wondering if what you have done or not done is the cause of your child's disability. Remember, language disorder is extremely complex—so much so that researchers and professionals in the field can still only propose theories and possible explanations, based on the research and knowledge of that time.

WHAT CAUSES LANGUAGE DISORDER?

To give you a better understanding of the condition, I have outlined below some of the current theories of language disorder. Between us, parents and professionals, we can decide whether or not we feel one, or any, or none of them makes sense in relation to 'our' child.

The Medical Theory

You may have heard the term 'neurological' without really understanding what it relates to or, for that matter, what it means. It is a term which is used to apply to the nervous system, our brain, spinal cord and nerves. Our brain is divided into two halves, called hemispheres. As far as we understand it, the left side deals primarily with language and logical thinking, and the right side with the more creative pursuits of life such as art, music and sculpture. I have used the word 'primarily' in connection with the left hemisphere because we understand that some aspects of language function are also located in the right hemisphere.

Two specific areas in the left hemisphere have been identified with different aspects of language function. The first, known as Wernicke's area, deals with the processing of incoming information, and the second, Broca's area, with formulating language and the motor aspects of movements needed for language. It is, of course, never quite as simple as this, because both the brain and language are so complex, and there are other parts of the brain adjacent to Wernicke's and Broca's areas which act as a link between them and are actively involved with other aspects of speech and language function. There are also links with other areas of the brain dealing with associated communication, such as gesture and facial expression.

The medical theory suggests that something has gone wrong within one or more parts of our neurological system, especially in those areas of the brain in the left hemisphere dealing specifically with language. We can only speculate on what the malfunction may be: possibly minimal damage, maybe immaturity—even with all the research that has taken place, we really do not know. Probably the best analogy we have nowadays is the computer. For those of you who are computer literate, the 'medical' theory suggests damage to or a malfunction of the hardware.

The 'Innate'/Inheritance Theory

How often have you heard someone say, 'It runs in the family'? Problems of various kinds are sometimes observed through several generations of one family. Some of you may be aware that specific difficulties with reading can be present in a particular family. The problem may only affect some members, perhaps miss a generation and emerge in a later one. It also happens with language problems. When we are taking a case history we always ask if anyone in the family has ever had any problems, and a parent will often recall how her mother, her aunt or uncle, even herself, were 'slow talkers', or 'couldn't say their sounds'. Speech and language therapists, with many years' experience, will have worked with such families, especially if they have been resident in the same district for a long time. One witty colleague once referred to the phenomenon as a 'dynasty of disorders'.

Some of you may recall seeing one such family profiled in a TV programme. In their case, a particular speech difficulty had affected the older members of the family—the grandmother, her son, and then subsequently all her grandchildren. In this particular case, the family had been investigated using strict scientific research procedures, providing evidence which has not readily been available until relatively recently. In the past, evidence of this kind has been anecdotal, relying, as I have suggested, on the reports of therapists who have known through experience that these families do exist. Continuing with our analogy of the computer, I think we could equate this particular phenomenon with a virus in the software, which is repeatedly passed on.

The Psycholinguistic Theory
We all know that a house requires a well-built, sturdy foundation if it is to support the walls, windows, roof and all the furniture that goes inside. It is just the same with language: to develop in the normal way, it too must have a foundation. Memory plays a very important part in our lives, for without it we really would be lost. How could we plan to do anything, or retain anything we had learned? It is an essential layer of our language foundation. We also need to be able to perceive all the incoming information in order to understand the relationships of things in the world around us, see, hear, retain and recall patterns. Attention plays an equally important role in language learning, for how could we possibly attempt to attend to the vast amount of information with which we are constantly bombarded if we did not organise it into manageable chunks, and filter out whatever was redundant?

We also need the ability to give meaning to symbols, such as words and speech sounds, to make associations between the real world and the language which represents it. This, along with the skills of attention, perception and memory, underpins language learning; if any one of them is not functioning in the normal way, then language learning will be affected.

Linguistic Theory
Lastly, there is the linguistic theory or perhaps more accurately *a* linguistic theory, since there is more than one to explain language disorder. Language can be thought of as

being made up of three 'parts' or aspects. These are: form, content and use. For language to function normally, it is dependent on the 'integration' or mix of these three. Briefly, by content we mean the words we use, the ideas they represent and how they all relate to each other and, in addition, the information and meaning conveyed by them in our language.

Form looks at the actual structure of our language. The sort of sounds we use in speech, and how they add meaning to our language depending on how they are used; how words combine one with another to give a particular structure to a sentence; also, how we use intonation, rhythm and stress to give greater meaning to our language. Put another way, it is how we say things, rather than what we say.

Use is exactly this: how we use language to interact with people, to obtain goals, to make sure that the language we choose accurately reflects the message we are sending—in other words, that it is understood by our listener. We don't talk to our children in the same way as we would to the bank manager. At least, we hope it wouldn't be necessary, for if it were, I and a host of others would quickly change our bank.

Our knowledge of form, content and use therefore underlies both the speaking and the understanding of our language. If one 'part' is missing, those that remain cannot work efficiently. Unless our computer has all its components or 'parts' working, with both the hardware and the programs used with the hardware, and unless there is a good interface, it will misinterpret our messages and give us the wrong information. (See Figure 10.)

EDUCATION FOR CHILDREN WITH LANGUAGE DISORDER

Depending on where you live, there will be a range of specialist pre-school provision—a special nursery, an assessment class or a special pre-school language class. Even so, not all children with language disorder receive this kind of

LANGUAGE DEVELOPMENT NEEDS THE SUCCESSFUL COMBINATION OF THESE THREE FACTORS

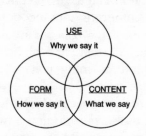

USE
Why we say it

FORM
How we say it

CONTENT
What we say

SOMETIMES THESE FACTORS DO NOT ALL FIT TOGETHER

The child has good ideas but is unable to express them in sentences.

FORM
How we say it

CONTENT
What we say

USE
Why we say it

The child has good sentences but lacks ideas.

CONTENT
What we say

FORM
How we say it

USE
Why we say it

The child knows what to say and how to say it, but not always at the right time.

USE
Why we say it

FORM
How we say it

CONTENT
What we say

Figure 10. Form, content and use.

Adapted from an original used by Southdowns Health (NHS) Trust.

intensive help, simply because there are not enough places to match the number of children. Occasionally, too, children may miss out for other reasons—ill health, difficult home circumstances or perhaps because their family has moved from place to place, never resident anywhere long enough for their child to receive regular help.

Whether or not they have received intensive therapy before going to school, some children will continue to have language difficulties so severe that they will need specialised help once they enter school. Unless this is available, they are likely to fail. Increasingly, Local Education Authorities are becoming aware of the special needs of this group of children and, even if they have no pre-school facilities, are now taking steps to provide for infant age children.

What facilities should you look for when you know your child has a very severe and specific language disability? At present, three main areas of provision exist for school age children with language disorder:

— Independent specialist language schools.

— Language units.

— Extra teaching and ancillary help in a mainstream class, with therapy in school provided by a speech and language therapist.

Children with disabilities such as blindness, deafness, physical disability, learning disability or emotional disturbance, have for decades been recognised as having special educational needs. However, this has not been the case with children who have language disorder: only in the 1940s were their needs officially acknowledged.

A Brief Look at History
It was the Education Act of 1944 that finally gave recognition to children with speech and language difficulties. Of course, they had always been there: speech therapy, then a relatively young profession, had for years been aware of the damaging

Help Me Speak

effect of language disorder on children's learning and had been campaigning for this to be recognised by Education Authorities. Children with 'speech defect', as it was then termed, became a new category of pupil in the 'Handicapped Pupils and School Service Regulations' in 1945, and took their place along with the ten other previously identified categories.

It quickly became clear that a number of children, those we now describe as having a language disorder, would need a very special type of education if they were not to continue failing. In 1948 the first school for children with language disorder was established, Moor House School in Oxted, Surrey, which took children on a residential basis. For the very first time in the United Kingdom, speech therapists and teachers worked together.

John Horniman School in West Sussex followed in 1958, and since then there has been a gradual but continuous expansion of these schools, from three in 1965 to eighteen in 1993.

We know now that there are far more children with language disorder in the school population than could possibly be accommodated in three special schools, and by 1965 this fact had become fairly obvious to Education Authorities. Understandably, not all parents were enthusiastic about the prospect of their young children attending residential schools; some form of specialist provision was needed at local level and language units were seen as the most sensible solution.

Perhaps the term 'language unit' is not the best one to use, for some parents become confused, imagining it to be a class in a special school, for children who are 'not very bright'. Language units, rather like the children in them, come in all shapes and sizes, with the majority located in mainstream schools. Provision across the country varies: some LEAs have a large number while neighbouring LEAs may have only one or two, or even, in some cases, none at all.

Although there are many units which provide education for children throughout the primary age range, LEAs still tend to give priority to the infant age range. Unfortunately, there are very few units for children of secondary age: if their speech and language disability persists beyond the primary level, children either go to a specialist residential school or are placed in their local school and provided with specialist teaching and therapy support. Currently, there are more than 300 language units throughout the country, and everyone is delighted that this number is increasing.

A number of LEAs have taken the decision fully to integrate children with special needs in regular classes within mainstream schools and this, of course, includes children with language disorder. In my opinion, using this particular 'model' of provision can place great strains on staff and children, especially if it is not well funded and well resourced by sufficient specialist staff. Several authorities, on the other hand, have responded to the needs of children with language disorder in innovative ways. Birmingham is one: here they have a visiting specialist teacher service. On the other hand, St Helen's, Merseyside, has employed speech and language therapists who are also qualified teachers, renaming them 'logopaedists', to provide a similar service.

Location of Language Units

Children with language disorder can gain a lot by mixing with normally speaking children, and for this reason most language units are located within mainstream schools. In an ideal world, there would be a unit in a local school close enough for parents to walk there with their children, but since this is not the case, children attending are transported by bus or taxi from a catchment area substantially larger than that of the school where the unit is based.

The actual location of a language unit within a school can make a big difference to how the children are accepted by the others. It is really far better for them to have their classroom in the main body of school, to encourage them to mix and generally be seen, rather than in one of those 'port-a-cabin' constructions, located somewhere outside.

Who Pays?

Before we go any further, it may be helpful to look at the sometimes confusing issue of funding for children with language disorder. Perhaps I should first explain that all schools are now given an amount of money under a system which enables them to hold their budget and spend it in whatever way they consider best for their needs. Language units are not included in this since each has a separate budget directly from the LEA, to pay for staff, equipment and so on.

So far that is all fairly straightforward. However, speech and language therapists are employed by the local Health Authority or Trust, and it is here that we find the greatest variation in sources of funding. Irrespective of whether the children are in a special class or integrated into mainstream, in some areas the health department pays for the therapist, whereas in others the work is wholly or partly funded by the LEA. I have yet to discover why such policy differences exist; perhaps it is, quite simply, that in the past there has been such a shortage of therapists that LEAs, rather than hoping that the Health Authority would eventually find enough money, have taken the decision to pay for the therapists themselves.

Specialist schools for children with language disorder are somewhat different: they are not funded from the state sector; they employ their own staff which, of course, includes speech and language therapists, and therefore the difficulty over who pays for therapy does not arise. Three of the schools, for example, come under the care of a charity, Invalid Children's Aid Nationwide (ICAN); many others are controlled by trust funds and rely on fund-raising for a significant proportion of their income. Of course, they also receive a substantial amount of money from fees paid by the LEAs who place children in their care.

Referral Procedures for Language Units and Specialist Schools

Parents will be consulted immediately if it is felt their child may be in need of the sort of intensive teaching and therapy provided in a language unit. Many parents have no idea what a language unit is and, quite honestly, why should they? It is our job as professionals to explain all the details and answer the numerous questions we are asked. For a child to attend a language unit is far from being a stigma, as was once suggested to me by a mum who had misunderstood what had been said to her. It is a positive if bewildering step in the life of any child and his family.

So how are children selected and referred for a language unit? Procedures vary across the country, but the following important steps are fairly typical. Usually, the first person to express concern about a child's severe communication disability is the therapist who is working with him. You will recall that the majority of children are referred for therapy quite early in their development, and only a minority fail to make the expected progress, owing to the very specific nature of their language impairment.

Of course, other professionals can and do refer children who, for one reason or another, have not previously been seen for therapy. Nowadays most children who are thought to need a place in a language unit are 'statemented'. So your child will be seen by a whole team of professionals—a therapist, a senior therapist, possibly the teacher who is the co-ordinator of the language unit, the educational psychologist and a clinical medical officer. Every child's name is placed on a waiting list for consideration at a meeting, which usually takes place once a term.

Children are selected on grounds of eligibility, priority and availability; there are no favourites, so rest assured that the merits of your child's case will have been fully discussed, even though on this occasion he may not have been successful because of a shortage of places. His eligibility will be considered at a later date.

Sarah was referred to the local clinic when she was three years old. She had excellent understanding of language, but only used the odd vowel sound and lots of expressive gesture. With therapy, she improved a little: she began to string together vowels and one or two consonants, but by now she was four and the therapist had already begun to express concern over the rate of her progress. Being a perceptive person, Sarah's mother was also wondering how Sarah would cope with a large class in school and, even more worrying, how she would learn with so little language. When the possibility of a language unit place was mentioned, Sarah's mother agreed immediately, expressing her relief that this special form of education existed for children like her daughter.

Patience is one of the first attributes parents must possess in order to ease their way through the somewhat protracted assessment process. The long list of very knowledgeable professional people who saw Sarah, in order to give their advice for her statement, thought she was an intelligent child, and this was confirmed by the psychologist's assessment. So, with the statementing procedure under way, Sarah could be discussed at the panel meeting, which was held once a term.

I have mentioned the difference in numbers of units across the country, with some areas boasting an abundance and others only one or two. Sarah did not have a choice as she lived in an area where only one unit had been established, with a maximum of two vacancies occurring in the near future. Sarah secured a place, but others were not so fortunate and even though the panel made constructive recommendations about the kind of help they should receive in the meantime, many parents felt their children had been deprived of the sort of education they desperately required.

Just occasionally, we work with children whose difficulties are so complex and severe that we know they will need specialised education and therapy for the foreseeable future. Many LEAs in the country simply do not maintain language units which cater for both the primary and secondary levels of education, and so, in consultation with the parents, those children are referred to independent specialist schools for children with language disorder. These schools, which are usually residential, are often the only alternative for children who fail to make progress in the language units. It is a big step in any family's life to send a child away to school; it is also expensive for the LEA, even for the few who can attend as day pupils. With fees ranging from £9,000 to £14,000 a year, everyone has to be very sure they are making the right decision for the child.

Staff at the specialist schools make their own searching and detailed assessment of the children before offering a place to them, as well as taking the advice of the professionals who have worked regularly with the children. Certainly no child will even be considered unless he already has a statement from his LEA, recommending that he should go to a specialist school. This is a commitment from the LEA that it would be prepared to pay for the child should he be accepted.

The majority of children like Sarah attend language units, and her experience of the unit is typical of many others in the United Kingdom, no matter where they happen to live. Some years ago, both the Invalid Children's Aid Nationwide (ICAN) and the Association for all Speech Impaired Children (AFASIC), published guidelines for language units, following a major piece of research which revealed little uniformity between existing units, with many working in contrasting ways. These guidelines have helped considerably not only in setting up new units, but also in improving those already in existence. Sarah's unit, for the infant age range of five to seven, fulfilled many of the recommendations for numbers of children and staffing. There were eight children, a full-time teacher and ancillary helper, and a part-time therapist. In order to encourage integration of the children with the rest of the school, the unit had deliberately been placed in the main building.

Sarah's parents were naturally curious to know how their daughter was going to be taught. How would it be possible to teach the National Curriculum, as well as teach the children to understand language and to speak? Language is needed for all kinds of learning and is essential for the large number of subjects taught in the National Curriculum. For children in the unit the day can seem very long with so much to achieve—much more than would be expected of any other child of a similar age.

Like many of the other children in the class, Sarah urgently needed a way of making herself understood and so was taught manual signing to accompany her incoherent attempts at speaking. She was thrilled. At last she could make everyone understand what she wanted; she could make a comment or ask a question. To the others in the class it was just as much of a revelation: they could actually see as well as hear language. One little boy expressed it very well when he said, 'My hands can talk with me now.'

Sarah needed something just as effective to help her with her incomprehensible speech, something which would give her visual hooks on which to hang those oh, so difficult speech sounds. There are several symbol systems in use by therapists, some more exciting than others. As Walt Disney discovered many years ago, children adore cartoon characters, and Sarah quite literally fell in love with the symbol system which I mentioned in Chapter 3, called 'Letterland', which has that magical cartoon-like quality about it. Therapists use Letterland to help children like Sarah with their speech, and teachers use it to teach phonics for reading and spelling.

Some children, however, find learning speech sounds so hard that not even Letterland, or any other symbol system in use, is sufficient to teach them speech sounds. An extra prop for their learning is provided through finger signs, referred to as 'cues', used to accompany spoken consonant and vowel sounds. The cues provide the children with essential information about the kind of sound they are attempting to make and where in their mouths the sounds are articulated.

For most of us, learning grammar for speech is not a process which requires any conscious thought: it just happens, as if by magic, when we are learning to speak. Sarah had not been touched by this magic; for her the grammar of her own language was just as difficult as that of a foreign language is for the rest of us. She only began to understand when she was introduced to what is known as colour coding, in which categories of language are given a colour. Sarah learned that nouns were orange words, verbs were yellow, adjectives green and so on. Colour acted as a kind of learning 'hook' on which to hang words, whilst the colour sequence taught her about word order. Simple written language presented in this way helped Sarah to string words together in a way that made sense.

Like many other children with specific language disorder, Sarah, was very clumsy; she found it almost impossible to manipulate a pencil or scissors, to a catch a ball, to jump, hop or skip. Close links with the local Health Authority meant that help was nearby, through a visiting occupational therapist and a physiotherapist. Between them they gave practical advice and programmes of exercises, which could be linked to the daily work of the unit.

With the expert teaching and therapy she received Sarah made excellent progress, and within six months was spending a small part of her day in a larger class in the school. So began the long, slow process of preparing her to go, eventually, to her local school, once her speech and language had sufficiently improved. She remained in the language unit for six terms, approximately 18 months, before finally wishing everyone goodbye.

We are often asked, by parents and fellow professionals, how long we think it will take for a child to improve. Mostly we can make an educated guess, but with certain children it is far from clear and we can only admit that we honestly do not know.

You may wonder how different it might be for a child if he attended an independent special school. They use many of the same techniques you see in a unit, the major difference being that they can devise their own curriculum, since independent schools are not subject to the National Curriculum. Perhaps I should add that, since the long-term aim of most special schools is to return children to their local school, they do have the National Curriculum in mind when teaching children.

Reflecting for a moment on children like Sarah and Chris, whom I mentioned at the beginning of this chapter, they are in a way the lucky ones, for they received the right kind of help at a critical time in their lives. For many children, this will not be the case. It is an increasing problem of insufficient places for children with language disorder. Although help was late in coming for Chris, it eventually materialised and he had the best that was available. He responded to it and is now enjoying the life and friendship of an understanding sixth form college—Chris who, at age five, said to his parents, 'Why did God only give me half brain?', and at age seven, 'I sometimes wonder if I'm really here or if I'm just a thought in Jesus' mind.'

5 Learning Difficulties

As we know, there are many reasons why children fail to learn language in the usual way, and inevitably it is a great source of concern to most parents that their child might be considered to be a slow learner. As often as not, when we are discussing a child's development, this fear is expressed— usually by a denial. I recall a mother who had delayed bringing her child to therapy until he was of school age and one of the first things she said was, 'I know he's not thick, I don't care what anyone else says, I just know it.'

Sometimes, as with this mother, it is one of the reasons why children are not brought to therapy at an early age. This is a great pity because, no matter what the cause, we can do so much to help at that critical pre-school age. Research shows that of all the children who attend the local clinic, a number will be found to have learning difficulties. This is apart from those children whose progress will have been monitored because, for one reason or another, they were identified at birth as being 'at risk'.

Even though they may have come to the attention of other agencies earlier, sooner or later they are likely to be seen by a speech therapist and, without doubt, a number of them will have learning difficulties.

Some, but not all, parents will be aware that it is not the responsibility of the therapist to decide whether or not a child has a learning difficulty, and you may rightly ask who, then, makes that decision. There are several professionals involved with very young children, the first usually being the clinical medical officer and the second the educational psychologist. Rest assured that speech and language therapists would never make any referral to another person without discussing it with parents first. It is only after working with a child for a while that we would begin to ask questions, for we will have noticed that Peter or Anna are making slow progress not only in their language development, but also in other areas of their learning.

What We Mean by Learning Difficulties

It is likely that we have all experienced difficulties in learning some subject or other when we were at school. It might have been maths, physics or Latin, and yet we were not considered to have a 'learning difficulty'. It is all a question of degree. How much a child fails to learn and the rate at which learning progresses are both indicators of whether he has a learning difficulty. Thank goodness, in these more enlightened days we no longer use derogatory terms to label an individual who learns slowly—for example, mentally defective, imbecile, feeble-minded, mentally retarded or mentally subnormal. 'Learning difficulty' is a broad term. Briefly, it can be analysed as follows:

— Specific learning difficulty: implies that the child has problems with one aspect of learning, such as reading.

— Moderate learning difficulty: the child is behind in most aspects of learning.

— Severe learning difficulty: the child may not progress as far as acquiring even the basic skills of life.

For simplicity, we can look upon learning difficulties as a continuum, a sort of continuous horizontal line: at one end there are few problems, and at the other the problems are severe:

Specific	Moderate	Severe
learning difficulty	learning difficulty	learning difficulty

Sooner or later the inevitable question is asked: what causes children to have learning difficulties? Often, the cause of a learning difficulty is obvious: it may have happened as a result of some damage to the brain, it may be due to disease or perhaps it is associated with a particular syndrome, such as Down's Syndrome.

From time to time, however, we work with families who have a history of learning difficulty running through several generations. These learning difficulties can be specific or even quite severe. You could, of course, speculate that this is no coincidence and that there has to be a genetic reason for it. Then there are the external conditions which can give rise to learning difficulties, such as social deprivation, neglect, abuse, emotional and behavioural disturbance. One can go on: prolonged illness or separation, the use of medication, hearing loss and bereavement are all factors which can interfere with a child's learning. Of course, there are always those children who fail to learn and we do not know the reason why. However, irrespective of the severity or the cause, it is the educational psychologist who can help us determine the nature of a child's problems.

The Educational Psychologist's Role in Learning Difficulties
You will recall from Chapter 3 how essential the educational psychologist is in helping therapists make decisions about the usefulness of therapy at a specific time in a child's life. How educational psychologists go about this has changed considerably in recent years. Not so long ago it was normal practice to give intelligence a numerical grading, known as the 'intelligence quotient' (IQ). By using this single measure individuals were graded, and educated accordingly. Many readers may recall the much discussed 11+ examin-

ation which relied solely on IQ as a measure of ability.

In recent years a wider range of assessments has become available and educational psychologists can now tell us more precisely in which aspects of learning a child is failing. One assessment, for example, looks at the following:

- Naming vocabulary.
- An aspect of auditory memory.
- Verbal reasoning.
- Speed of understanding or processing information.
- Number skills; and matrices.

With so much more information, the educational psychologist can obtain a far more accurate profile of a child's learning compared to the old overall IQ, which gave us little idea of a child's strengths and weaknesses. In addition, these kind of assessments give us some indication of how a child is learning in comparison with other children.

Therapists need to know whether a child's delayed language is at a similar stage of development to his other skills, in order to decide whether or not he really needs therapy. If in every other way a child at the age of four years was just like a two-year-old, it would not be unusual for his language to be at a two-year level.

It is equally essential, when there is a more specific problem with language, for therapists to have this kind of information. Educational psychologists use assessments which make this distinction: some items will rely on language for problem solving, while others will not. You may well remember Rubic's cube. Everyone seemed to possess one a few years ago, and it did not require language to achieve the final pattern. It is the same with the block design and patterns used by educational psychologists in their assessments. Those test items which require language are referred to as 'verbal', and those which do not as 'non-verbal'. Therapists would quite naturally be very concerned if there was a wide difference between these two scores—in other words, if the non-verbal score was high and the verbal score low. So you can see that, in certain circumstances, therapists need the support of their educational psychology colleagues for guidance.

Katie and David, both aged three-and-a-half, were two children who benefited enormously from the assessment and advice of the educational psychologist. Without his help, therapists would still be wondering if their observations of the children were accurate. Both children attended a pre-school language group, and as far as the therapists could judge they had very similar problems, understanding very little and only uttering a few unintelligible sounds.

At this point the therapists' observations showed how the similarity ended. Katie was a busy little bee, pursuing other children and insisting, in her very limited language, that they join her in the play-house. At times, when her language failed, she would forcibly drag them to where she wanted them to play her game. David spent much of his time, if allowed, wandering around somewhat aimlessly, holding a toy but making no effort to play with it. He appeared to have little idea what it was for, and related very little with the other children. Generally, the world seemed a rather alien and confusing place for him. When both children were assessed by the educational psychologist, the therapists' observations and concerns were justified. Katie had a very specific difficulty with learning language, whereas David was delayed in all areas of his learning, including language.

Who Needs Speech and Language Therapy?
If we look at the 40 per cent statistic referring to children in special schools, who need help from speech and language therapists at some time in their school career, it quickly becomes apparent that we need to be absolutely clear when, and how often, during this period, therapy will be most effective. Remember, this figure does not include all those children with learning difficulties who attend ordinary schools. Many of these children will, of course, have been referred

to therapy before they went to school and perhaps have already received substantial help.

If children have learning difficulties they are likely to be slow in learning language, and it is only when there is a specific problem with communication that therapists will become involved. I believe there is some confusion over this distinction, not only with parents, but also sometimes with our professional colleagues. Our general rule in making decisions about help, or intervention as we call it, is whether or not a child has a specific difficulty with one or more aspects of his communication. We would suggest, perhaps with some justification, that if this is not the case, and his language development is appropriate to his other skills, the expert help of speech and language therapists is not what is needed. If, in all ways, he is, say, just like an eighteen-month-old child, even though he is six years of age, we would not see it as necessary for us to give therapy.

In cases like this we would, however, give support and advice on the normal development of language in a variety of other ways, by working with parents or professional colleagues, such as teachers. I think the phrase mentioned in the statistic above, 'at some time in their school career', summarises how therapists work. Our aim is for every child to make progress, and like all concerned professionals we want to know that what we are doing is effective. It is only by careful monitoring and reassessment that we can judge when a child has progressed sufficiently to require no further help—at least, at that particular time in his life. So you can see that, for many children, therapy will be required intermittently throughout the whole of their school lives, which is hardly surprising when you consider how the demands on a child's language increase as he progresses through school.

Some children with severe learning difficulties may never acquire spoken language or, if they do, it may be so poor that they will need to use augmentative communication systems. These are other forms of communication, such as signing, which I shall be discussing in detail in the next chapter. In this instance, a therapist may decide that once she has assessed what is needed by a child and set up a programme, the day-to-day work can be done just as well by others who are in daily contact with the child.

EDUCATIONAL PROVISION

In order to explain what speech and language therapists do for children with learning difficulties, it is essential to be aware of where the children receive their education, since this usually influences how we work. For all children, the opportunity to learn can never begin soon enough. For children with learning difficulties, it is possibly even more important that they have organised help as early as possible in their lives. Ideally many children with learning difficulties will have had the chance to attend one of the specialist pre-school classes discussed in Chapter 3. Whether this was full-time or part-time is really irrelevant, so long as they were able to benefit from the right kind of teaching and therapy from an early age.

When children reach school age, it is then that decisions will have to be made. Will a child's needs best be met in special school or unit, or at the local primary school? For those children whose learning difficulties have already been recognised, a document called a 'statement of need' may have been prepared by the Local Education Authority (LEA), which outlines the problems a child is experiencing and what he will need, in educational terms, to deal with them.

Speech and language therapists are invited to send a report on the child if he has been receiving therapy, along with everyone else who has been working with him. However, it is important to remind parents that they are consulted throughout, as well as being invited to write a report themselves.

Only a relatively small number of children with learning

difficulties actually go to a special unit or school, since the majority are educated in mainstream school where the organisation exists to deal with their problems. Every school has a skilled member of staff, a 'special needs co-ordinator'—usually someone with a great deal of teaching experience—who has the responsibility of assessing and devising special programmes for the children. It is a stimulating appointment that entails giving advice to other staff members as well as supervising untrained people, known as non-teaching aids or ancillaries, who are employed to work with the children in class.

Of course, some of these children will require therapy, so therapists will either see them at the local clinic, maintaining close contact with school staff and in particular the special needs co-ordinator, or will visit the school regularly in order to work more closely with children and teachers.

Some children will go straight to special schools, with the agreement of parents and the LEA, whilst occasionally, children from mainstream schools are transferred. Sometimes, even after all the hard work of teachers, children and parents, it becomes increasingly apparent that the mainstream school may not be meeting a child's needs and alternative schools will have to be considered.

Special Schools
Although many children with learning difficulties attend mainstream schools, others, because of the complexity or severity of their disability, will go to a special school. However, following the 1981 Education Act, some LEAs disbanded their special schools, using the teachers and money saved to improve facilities for special needs children in mainstream schools. Most authorities still prefer to keep the option of educating children with certain complex disabilities in separate schools, whilst at the same time being flexible enough to return children to mainstream whenever it is in the best interests of the child.

What kinds of special school are available for children

with learning difficulties? Children may go to what is called an MLD (moderate learning difficulty) school or alternatively an SLD (severe learning difficulty) school. Most schools take children aged between five and sixteen, but where there is a large number of children two schools may be needed, one at the primary level and one at the secondary level. In the past, the decision for a child to be sent to one or the other, MLD or SLD, depended on a child's IQ score, which was supposedly a measure of his intelligence. Keep in mind that 100 is the figure that represents the 'average': so if the child's score was between 50 and 75 he was sent to the MLD school; if it was 50 or lower, he went to the SLD school.

Nowadays, decisions about where a child should be educated are far more flexible, depending much more on what is best for the child at a particular time in his life. For example, children who go to MLD schools are there because they are failing to learn for a variety of reasons. Small classes and the specialist help available may, in time, make it possible for a child to improve enough to return to mainstream school.

All children who go to a special school must have a statement which is regularly reviewed, usually once a year. Parents are included in this discussion of their child's progress; moreover, these meetings provide an ideal opportunity for everyone to discuss the child's future.

Occasionally, children with difficulties of a different kind may find their way into MLD schools, for a variety of reasons—for example, as a result of a child moving from one part of the country to another. At the age of five-and-a-half years, Jamie was a puzzling little boy who had come into a local MLD school from another LEA; he was a very difficult, unco-operative child with unusual learning difficulties. He refused to co-operate with any formal assessments and withdrew into silence, behaviour which no amount of bribing could persuade him to change. Gradually, the teachers and therapist won his confidence and he began to communicate, but even so it took over a year to get a true picture of his abilities.

Eventually everyone discovered what it was that Jamie had wanted so desperately to hide. He knew his speech was awful, so poor that he only had a total of two consonants and an unreliable range of vowels, and his co-ordination was so inadequate that drawing and writing were equally difficult. No wonder he frequently told people to 'i o'—his way of using the mild invective 'piss off'. In fact, Jamie was not in the right place for his particular difficulties, but had he not had the opportunity of working with a range of specialist teachers and a therapist, it would have taken a great deal longer to discover his abilities.

Speech and Language Therapists Working in MLD and SLD Schools
As I explained in Chapter 4, even though some therapists may be working for the majority of their time in schools, they are not actually employed by the LEA. This is a situation which can lead to a great deal of confusion. It is even further complicated because of the variety of ways in which some LEAs and Health Authorities have agreed to fund the work. In some instances, the LEA has agreed wholly to fund the posts, whilst in others there is a joint arrangement, with both authorities contributing equal amounts.

Either way, in most areas the money is handled by the senior therapist for the district, and the responsibility for management of staff remains with the speech and language therapy department. It is not as complex as it first appears. Since 1974, the health department has provided staff for all special schools and units in the state educational system, which continues to exist in many areas. It is only in recent years that ideas have changed, mainly in response to a shortage of funds on both sides.

The decision about how much therapy time is allocated to each school is made by the District Speech and Language Therapy Manager, in consultation with the schools. Where funding is shared, it would also be with the LEA. Parents are sometimes perplexed by the differences in the amount of therapy provided in one area compared to another, regardless of schools being within the same LEA. This is explained by the number of different Health Authorities or Trusts which are in the boundaries of the LEA, and the variation of priorities each may have for its population.

Being in a school is rather different from working any-where else. In a school, a therapist is regarded as a member of staff, rather than the visiting specialist who regularly comes to take a clinic. Even so, staff in MLD and SLD schools vary considerably in their understanding and know-ledge of the role of the speech and language therapist within their team. In a way, this is understandable, for it is rare for a school to have the full-time services of a therapist. It is not an easy role for the therapist, who must show tact and discretion in explaining what she does, whilst at the same time fulfilling the high expectations of the schools. I suspect that all professionals who are part-time members of staff experience the same kind of pressure to condense the equivalent of one week's work into half the time.

Whatever we do as therapists, summarised in Figure 11, harmony with other professionals is most important. How-ever, despite our best efforts to inform, some teachers have a peculiar idea of what we do, which I thought we had suc-cessfully dispelled.

Differences Between Working in MLD and SLD Schools
For therapists, the actual duties undertaken will not be sig-nificantly different, whether they are working in an MLD or an SLD school. The major difference will be in the intel-lectual level of the children. In practice, this means that, at the SLD school, perhaps more children will be at a pre-linguistic stage of development and greater emphasis will need to be placed on communication skills, as opposed to speech and language skills. Think of the young baby who is in the first year of life, and the way in which he

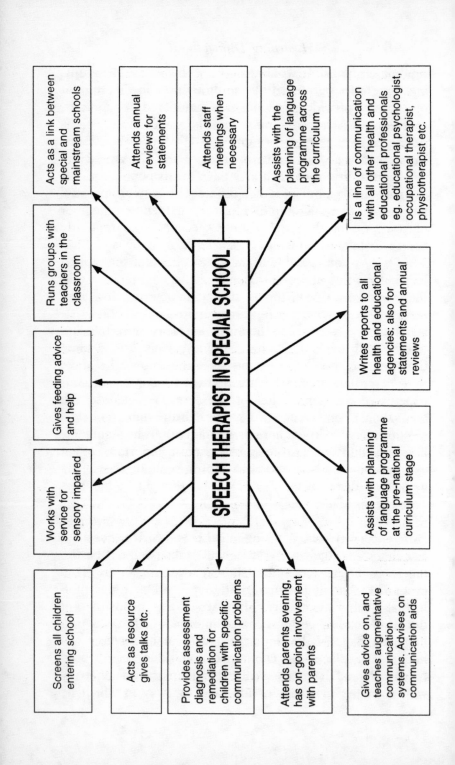

SPEECH THERAPIST IN SPECIAL SCHOOL

Acts as a link between special and mainstream schools

Attends annual reviews for statements

Attends staff meetings when necessary

Assists with the planning of language programme across the curriculum

Is a line of communication with all other health and educational professionals eg. educational psychologist, occupational therapist, physiotherapist etc.

Runs groups with teachers in the classroom

Gives feeding advice and help

Works with service for sensory impaired

Screens all children entering school

Acts as resource gives talks etc.

Provides assessment diagnosis and remediation for children with specific communication problems

Attends parents evening, has on-going involvement with parents

Gives advice on, and teaches augmentative communication systems. Advises on communication aids

Assists with planning of language programme at the pre-national curriculum stage

Writes reports to all health and educational agencies: also for statements and annual reviews communicates without language as you and I know it, and you will appreciate the sort of skills these children will need to be taught. Then again, there may well be more children who have multiple disabilities and may never achieve speech; they would be using augmentative communication systems such as signing, picture boards or other symbol boards. Nor must we forget that there is an ever-increasing number of children who need help with feeding and the control of dribbling.

Language in the Curriculum
With the introduction of the National Curriculum, all our lives changed to a greater or lesser degree, professionals' as well as parents'. Teachers are now far more aware that they must pay a great deal more attention to a child's speaking and listening, for they are now expected to assess and teach these skills. It is my experience that teachers in MLD and SLD schools have been aware of the need for the schools to have some guidelines on the teaching of spoken language (what they would call a 'policy'), but have not always found time to plan and put it into practice. Because so many children in these schools have delayed language development, it is vital that spoken language is taught, for unlike other children they do not necessarily learn language simply by being exposed to it.

So the therapist's role has been to assist teachers to augment a spoken language programme for all children throughout the school. Today, to overcome the complexities of the language demanded by the National Curriculum, resourceful therapists working in SLD schools have devised a language programme, in preparation for it.

As a parent you are probably wondering if there is any difference between the assessments we use in schools and those we use in a clinic. There is no difference; but not only that, the whole approach to assessment is very similar. However, the approaches we use for therapy can differ, as with the cases of Susie and Rod.

Susie was a bright-eyed six-year-old when I first saw her. Over the years, for some unexplained reason, she had become a disturbed and destructive little girl. At that time she was in an MLD school. On one occasion, by a series of violent tantrums, Susie had all but destroyed her classroom, apparently for no other reason than not being able to have her own way.

Unfortunately, Susie's frustration was made worse by her very limited language, which no one could understand. I decided that, since her understanding of language was in keeping with her other skills, she was capable of learning an augmentative communication system in order to communicate her immediate needs and bring down her level of frustration. A simple hand-signing system, Makaton, was introduced and used in the classroom as well as in therapy. In fact everybody joined in—the other children in the class, the teachers, the ancillaries, Susie's mum and dad and even the dinner ladies. It was great fun. Susie loved being able to make herself understood and, at the same time, the centre of attention. From being a quite unmanageable child, her behaviour changed dramatically to becoming a little girl who was relaxed, yet retained a normal childlike naughtiness.

Much to my delight, Susie's language began to improve and, at the stage when she was putting four and five words together, I felt she was confident enough for us to do some specific therapy on speech sounds. At this stage she had very little idea of how words fitted together in sentences; she frequently missed out small words like 'a' and 'is', and on top of that, she didn't always say the words in the right order. Although signing helped her with this, Susie needed another prop for her memory, so, as she had just begun to read, we introduced her to colour coding, which I outlined in Chapter 4 when I was discussing Sarah. Suddenly, everything began to make sense.

Susie found speech sounds difficult to remember, especially their order in words. What came first, second and last was a bit of a mystery, until we began to play all kinds of games in which she had to recall order. The order of objects in a row, pictures, musical sounds and, hardest of all—speech sounds. Susie couldn't say the sounds very accurately, either; so as well as practising them in words, she needed lots of practice with her tongue and lips. She had continued signing to make herself understood, but as her speech became clearer, Makaton was no longer necessary and she eventually stopped using it.

Without the combined efforts of everyone who worked with Susie and knew her, I doubt if she would have made such significant progress with her speech and language. Most certainly her antisocial behaviour would have been a problem for far longer. She required a great deal of individual help for her speech, which continued for nearly two years.

Not every child requires such an intensive approach. Rod, an amiable twelve-year-old, had been given a great deal of help over the years for his speech and language. This had improved beyond all recognition, yet socially he still retained certain problems. He did not always know how to react to people; he was awkward and self-conscious; and his blatant refusal to speak on occasions was sometimes interpreted as rudeness. On the brink of adolescence he felt socially vulnerable.

We must never forget that children who learn language in the normal ways have lots of practice, at the right time in their lives, to acquire all the skills of talking to other people. For children with speech and language difficulties, this practice is frequently denied. Usually, their attempts have been greeted with 'say that again' so many times that they have given up trying to communicate, except to those people they know really well.

Rod was not the only youngster in his class who was poor at talking and making relationships with other people. Others had similar problems but for different reasons. Working with the teacher, it was possible to set up a number of groups, in which the children had the opportunity to practise these skills, under the supervision of the teacher.

At first Rod's teacher wanted to know which situations the children found most frightening when they were talking. With some encouragement, they began to tell her: 'on the phone', 'talking to teacher', 'asking questions in class', 'asking for a fare on a bus or train', 'shopping', 'talking to someone of the opposite sex'. With this information, she asked the children to watch her having a chat with one of the class, to see if they could 'spot the mistakes'. She wanted them to become aware of what we need to do, in order to communicate successfully with others—such as eye contact, body distance, when to look and when to look away; how loudly to speak, how long to speak for, when to interrupt, and how to judge the level of difficulty of what you say to the other person.

The children thought this role-playing great fun, and over a period of many months had the opportunity to practise the numerous skills they needed, in the security of school. Eventually, the teacher persuaded them to try out their new-found skills in real-life situations—perhaps the toughest test of all. For the teacher it was a totally different way of working, but all along she had the support of the therapist.

By now you will appreciate that remediation for your child does not necessarily take place in isolation. It is the professional guidance and expertise of a highly skilled group of professionals that is frequently responsible for the child's eventual progress. Today, so many demands are placed upon the therapist that it would be impossible for her to devote all her time to seeing children on an individual basis; neither is it always desirable or in the best interests of the child, for with a group therapy approach there may well be greater progress. So it is the old maxim of 'horses for courses'. With anything from 25 to 75 per cent of a school's population in need of the therapist's help, within the team philosophy this approach is not only time-effective but, more importantly, it could be regarded as being more beneficial for the children.

Children with Feeding Difficulties

Certain children, especially those who have very severe learning difficulties as well as some other disability, may also suffer from problems with sucking, chewing and swallowing. There may only be a few children like this in any one school, but you can appreciate that the best and most convenient time to give advice on feeding techniques is at lunch. As most parents will understand, these children need to be weaned gradually from sloppy food to textured food, and finally to solids which require a great deal of chewing.

And what is the effectiveness of all this? Quite simply, it means improved muscle control and dexterity of the child's lips and tongue. All of this is vital, in order for the child to learn the movements needed to make speech sounds coherently. Just occasionally, there is a child who dribbles, which may be socially acceptable at two years of age, but not at seven. Neither is it a pleasant experience for the child. Without systematic help, you must be aware that this problem is unlikely to remedy itself.

The Makaton Signing System

The great joy of the Makaton signing system, used in many MLD and SLD schools, is its limited vocabulary and the simplicity of the signs. Many of the children have extremely poor body control, and the signs do not require good hand co-ordination. It also provides a very useful support for spoken language, as it is possible to combine signs to make short but accurate phrases. Sometimes Makaton is not sufficient, and the child may require a system which is simpler and uses symbols instead of signs.

Specific Learning Difficulty

The term 'specific learning difficulty' has become a euphemism for children who have particular problems with literacy or, more precisely, reading, spelling and writing. The term 'dyslexia' has been used to describe this condition, and for some years now there has been a great deal of controversy over whether such a condition exists. Speech therapists have become increasingly involved with this group of children, as a result of the research undertaken which clearly identifies the link between early spoken language difficulties and subsequent problems with written language. We are asked to assess children, usually by educational psychologists who have already seen the children and observed persisting speech or language difficulties.

Richard was a delightful eight-year-old, who was referred for an assessment by his mother; as a teacher, she knew Richard was experiencing some problems with his reading, which his school refused to acknowledge. As he had attended therapy some years previously and she noticed that he now did not always express himself fluently, his mother wondered whether there was a link between this and his reading difficulties.

When the therapist came to assess Richard, it was discovered that he had one significant deficiency in his language: he could not easily retrieve words. We all experience this from time to time, but for Richard it happened frequently. So, for instance, when he was reading he could not easily predict what words would be coming, which is something we all learn to do when we are reading. Fluent readers do not read every word. Rather, they use their language experience to predict words they do not look at. The therapist contacted the school and explained Richard's unusual difficulty with spoken language, and gave both school and parents strategies to teach to Richard, which would help him overcome it.

The background to this particular strategy was something like this. Words fall into different classes according to the numbers of them. Nouns (names of things), for example, are infinite in number and are therefore regarded as an 'open class', whereas prepositions (position words) are a 'closed class', because there are so few of them. If you think about it, a word from an open class is far harder to retrieve than one from a closed class, since there is a potentially infinite choice. The fewer the choices, the easier it is to retrieve.

Strategies, then, tend to focus primarily on the retrieval of nouns, which in Richard's case were his greatest problem. The following was suggested to his teacher:

- Use a core vocabulary, commonly used words and words from the current class topic.
- Think and write down all the attributes of the word—shape, size, colour, weight, smell, taste, feel.
- What is the function of the word—for example, do you throw it, eat it, sit on it, and so on?
- Where were you when you last saw it, and who were you with and what did they say?
- Visualise it and then try to draw it.
- Write down as many words as possible, that have the same meaning as this word.
- Write down all the words that are associated with it.
- Think of the sound it begins with and write down as many words as you can beginning with the same sound.
- Play games in which you have to guess missing words in a sentence (known as closure).
- Play games in which you describe an object and your partner has to guess what it is. Take turns.
- Play 'Kim's game'.
- Play 'I spy'.

Not every child's difficulties are so easily solved. Just occasionally, because their literacy is extremely poor, children fail so badly that they can no longer cope in mainstream and eventually move to an MLD school, where they have the benefit of small groups and more specialist teachers. Once in a while, children will be sent to special independent schools which specialise in dyslexia, and many of these employ their own therapists or buy in help as and when they need it.

The communication problems of children with learning difficulties are far from simple. They encompass anything from a minor difficulty with articulation, to virtually no

useful language. We must always remind ourselves that a
learning difficulty does not mean these children are
incapable of learning. Every child, no matter how limited
his ability, can learn something. Speech and language therapists, aware of this, use their skills not only with those children who have specific communication problems as well as
learning difficulties, but also with all the other children who
need to be taught language in order to learn it. We must
never underestimate what a child is capable of achieving,
for there have been many eight-year-olds labelled as failures,
who as adults are surprisingly successful.

6   Physical Disability

Even though they were both so small and had to fight
for survival at first, it never occurred to us that either
of our twins, born two months prematurely, would
actually be damaged or handicapped in any way. The
only problem we anticipated was having two babies
smaller than others and needing to catch up in terms
of their weight. Time was to dash our optimism. We
knew how ill Sarah had been, how she had stopped
breathing, and as she developed it became increasingly
apparent how different she was from her twin.

For parents, this kind of situation is a shattering experience.
Physical disability is not just the child's problem, it is one
which has far-reaching effects on the whole family. In
Sarah's case, her parents at least knew what had caused their
daughter's disability, but that vexed question, 'how did it
happen?', cannot always so easily be answered. We do
know, however, that damage to the brain can occur at any
time during a child's development—in the womb, at birth,
just after birth, and any time in its young life for a variety
of reasons.

   There is also a whole range of other conditions which will
cause a physical disability, usually genetically related. To go
into great detail would be outside the purpose of this book.
Nevertheless, some causes that are familiar and more readily
recognisable are worth mentioning. German measles,
for example, is a mild disease which, under normal

circumstances, would have very little effect other than a mild
degree of discomfort and a slight rash. When contracted in
the first few months of pregnancy, the opposite is true: the
disease can be devastating to the developing child (foetus)
and a multitude of handicaps can result—blindness, deafness
and severe brain damage. Until a child begins to develop,
we have no way of knowing precisely how damage of this
severity is going to affect physical and mental development.
There are other, well-documented but less well-known, diseases whose effects will be similar.

You will no doubt have read or heard about genetic disorders, those conditions known to be inherited, which can
cause anything from mild to severe physical disability. Many
of these are instantly identifiable at birth, because of their
distinct characteristics. It would be impossible, for example,
to miss children with the condition known as 'brittle bone
disease', particularly when it is severe, as they will be born
with bone deformities; whereas other conditions become
apparent as a child develops, and muscular dystrophy is perhaps one of the better known of these.

Drugs and alcohol abuse during pregnancy can be equally
destructive. They can bring about all kinds of brain damage
and a variety of physical deformities. In the last ten years a
new disease has found its way into our consciousness, and
it is a sad fact that an increasing number of children is being
born with the HIV virus or AIDS. Any severe head injury
may result in damage to the brain—you will hear the term
'trauma' or, to be more precise, the medical term, 'acute
neurological trauma'.

There are many more. It would be misleading to suggest
that every child with a physical disability also has a communication difficulty. Some forms of physical disability have no
effect on speech or language at all; a child born with one or
several limbs missing is unlikely to have any difficulties. We
know, however, that with many kinds of physical disability,
as often as not, speech and language are impaired in some
way, but exactly how depends very much on the cause of

the problem, and the circumstances surrounding it. There are children who are so severely affected by their physical disability that they cannot speak at all and have to be given another means of communication, whilst others have very little noticeable impairment.

CLEFT PALATE

Although not always regarded as a physical disability, cleft lip and palate is, nevertheless, a very obvious congenital deformity; more often it appears without any other complicating conditions, but it is sometimes associated with more complex syndromes. Cleft means a split or separation of parts, and it is during the early stages of pregnancy that separate areas of the face develop individually and then join together. If certain parts do not join properly, the result is a cleft lip or palate. It does not necessarily mean that any part is missing, although there is sometimes a lack of tissue.

Nowadays the condition can frequently be dealt with so successfully, at an early stage, that no speech or language difficulties are detectable as the child develops. Some children's problems, however, are not so easily rectified and those early operations are just the beginning of many that may well continue throughout his life. This is no one's fault, I hasten to add, but is related to the extent and complexity of the deformity.

One common complication associated with cleft lip and palate is that of hearing difficulty, which can also disrupt the development of spoken language. Most commonly, however, it is speech which is most severely affected. It's hard enough, as we know, trying to speak when we have just lost a tooth or two, but imagine attempting to articulate speech sounds without having the right amount of tissue in your mouth. This is the situation that daily confronts some children with cleft palate, at various stages during the reconstruction of their mouths.

Equally, if a child's soft palate (that's the bit that goes up and down at the back of your mouth when you say 'aah') is either too short or not working properly, it does not produce an effective seal between mouth and nose. Air escapes down the child's nose and, since he cannot create enough pressure in his mouth, all the sounds will be produced 'down his nose'. In this case, speech is very nasal and extremely difficult to understand. Feeding can also be uncomfortable, as both solids and liquids are likely to find their way back out through the child's nose. Nowadays, many clever devices called prostheses can help and may prevent this happening; they act in a crude way to fill up the gap and assist both feeding and speech.

Charlie was born with bilateral (that means both sides) cleft of lip and palate. He was referred for speech and language therapy at three-and-a-half years with delayed language development, pronunciation problems and nasal speech. Because of a lack of tissue, it had not been possible at an early stage completely to repair his palate; gradually this would be rectified through a series of operations as he grew older. With help, Charlie's language development progressed well, but although some progress was made with his pronunciation, it was limited by his remaining structural problems. Over the years, with successive operations and regular therapy, Charlie's speech has gradually improved. Now aged 14 years, he still has some difficulties with speech sounds, but what is most important is that he can be easily understood.

CEREBRAL PALSY

Some of you will be familiar with this particular term, as it is regularly mentioned on radio and TV. It is not, as one might think, a single condition; rather, it is a term which is used to describe a disorder of posture and movement. As far as we know, it is permanent and irreversible, caused by damage to, or under-development of, the brain before or around birth, but we also know that as the child matures and grows, changes will take place which from time to time can confound us. On more than one occasion, parents have been told their child will never walk, talk or be anywhere near normal; but fortunately, and to their great joy, these predictions have not always been accurate. To be fair to parents, we must be honest and realistic about their children's future, without losing the essential quality of optimism. As soon as a child is diagnosed as having the condition, therapy for the children and advice for parents are available from a team of professionals.

Although the workings of the brain remain one of the great mysteries of science, research tells us that when damage or maldevelopment (referred to as a lesion) occurs, as in cerebral palsy, the damage rarely affects just that area dealing with posture and the control of movement. The actual structure and function of other areas are frequently involved, which can affect learning, sight, hearing, speech and language and sometimes cause epilepsy.

It is an alarming fact, but in spite of much improved care of mothers and children during pregnancy and birth, the incidence of cerebral palsy is not falling; it has remained at about two in every 1,000 live births. Amongst professionals, it is well known that, in the majority of conditions we see in children, males are more commonly affected than females. Visit any special school, language unit or child development centre and the evidence is there—you don't really need a statistic to inform you. It is no different in the case of cerebral palsy: of those who have the condition, 55 per cent are male compared to 45 per cent female. Experts tell us that approximately 50 per cent of all people with cerebral palsy are of average intelligence, six per cent are of superior intelligence, 25 per cent have a moderate degree of learning difficulty and the remaining 19 per cent have severe learning difficulties. Surprisingly, in my experience most people are unaware of these statistics, believing incorrectly that every person with a physical disability such as cerebral palsy is also intellectually impaired.

Types of Cerebral Palsy

Just like other children, no one child with cerebral palsy is like another; each is an individual with his or her own particular difficulties. Nevertheless, professionals working with children suffering from cerebral palsy can identify patterns of disability to which, for convenience, they attach a label. Since cerebral palsy is associated with posture and movement, it is by observing the particular difficulties a child is experiencing with these that we obtain clues to the form of cerebral palsy he may have; those patterns we identify can be traced to lesions of particular parts of the brain.

Anyone who was unfamiliar with cerebral palsy would be rather surprised to learn that there are three forms of the condition which are clearly recognisable, and with each the speech of the children will usually be impaired, to a greater or lesser degree. It is probably the largest group, those with what is termed 'spastic' cerebral palsy, with whom most people are familiar. Of all those children who have cerebral palsy, approximately 70 per cent form the spastic group. One of the most distinctive characteristics of spasticity, which I am sure you will recall, is how abnormally tense and tight the children's muscles can become, caused by an increase in tone in the affected muscles. Because of the lesion in the child's brain, the muscles are receiving incorrect messages and therefore behave in an unusual way.

With their need to have order, professionals have yet another way of categorising spasticity, and by looking even more closely, we can see how different parts of the body can be involved. If the whole body is affected, the term 'quadriplegia' is used as a description: translated it literally means all four parts of your body. 'Hemiplegia' indicates involvement down either one side or the other of the body, 'hemi' meaning half, and 'diplegia' the bottom half of the body; 'di' meaning two. These descriptions do not mean exclusion of other muscles in the body, but indicate that this is primarily where the difficulties lie.

Janet had spastic quadriplegia, which meant she had

increased tone in the muscles over her entire body and this, of course, included muscles important for producing speech—those of the chest controlling breathing for speech, for producing voice from the larynx or 'voice box', muscles in the neck, mouth, tongue and face. It was a tremendous effort for her to control her muscles sufficiently to make herself understood. Janet was fortunate in that she had received intensive help for her speech from an early age. Through her own tenacity and effort, she was able to make herself understood, even though her voice was mostly too loud, and produced in short sharp bursts, sounding tense and stressed. It was not surprising that her pronunciation was not always clear.

As long as she stayed calm, Janet was a marvellous communicator regardless of her obvious speech and voice difficulties. Excitement caused spasm in her muscles and as a result her speech became incoherent. Being a tenacious person, in order to remind herself to remain calm, she eventually had a label made which read, 'I must not get excited', and attached it to her wheelchair!

Tim, on the other hand, had a rather different set of problems, which to the uninformed might look and sound similar to Janet's. Closer observation, however, revealed a great many differences. Tim had the form of cerebral palsy known as 'athetosis', from which 20–25 per cent of children with cerebral palsy suffer. With this, muscles are in a constant state of movement, a writhing, circular type of movement which makes the child appear to be in perpetual motion. Whether the child is at rest or attempting to move, the writhing movements continue, increasing in intensity when the child makes a voluntary movement.

Again, muscles concerned with speech are affected. It makes lip and tongue control very difficult, in order to produce the complex movements needed, firstly, for feeding and, secondly, for speech sounds. Co-ordinating movements of the lips, tongue and voice to achieve the right sequence for speech production is also extremely problematical (facial grimaces are common). So Tim had to learn to control the involuntary movements as best he could, in order to breathe, feed, swallow, produce voice and speak. In athetosis, voice is usually tense and comes in short bursts, so speech itself also tends to come in short bursts. Invariably it is slow, due to this lack of control. Like the speech of spastic individuals, it does not have normal rhythms and intonations.

One other form of cerebral palsy, from which only about five per cent suffer, is known as 'ataxic cerebral palsy'. Muscle control is again affected, but in a rather different way from either spasticity or athetosis. Watch a child walking who has ataxia and you might feel he resembles a sailor on the way home after a good night with his shipmates. Feet are wide apart and gait is 'staggering'. Unlike the drunken sailor, the person with ataxia is unco-ordinated over his whole body, and any movement will appear to be jerky and uncontrolled. Muscles used for feeding and speaking are affected as much as any others in the body, interfering not only with all the movements needed to produce voice, speech sounds and the intonations for speech, but also with sequencing them in order to create coherent words and sentences.

It is a sad but true fact that children's problems do not always come in neat, identifiable packages such as I have described, owing to the unpredictable nature of the condition. It is far more usual to find other complicating factors. The difficulties of communication that I have outlined should in theory be primarily associated with feeding, voice and speech, rather than with the understanding and formulation of language; sometimes, however, the learning of language itself can be a problem. This is often through lesions to those areas of the brain dealing with language. As we shall see later, lack of the normal opportunities for acquiring language can also have a harmful effect on language development.

When he was a year old George had meningitis, which left him partially paralysed down the whole of the right side of his body. This was an indication that he might well have difficulties with language, since, through one of those strange quirks of nature, nerve fibres from one side of the body cross over to the opposite side of the brain. As I explained in Chapter 4, we know from research that language function is regarded as being located primarily in the left-hand side of the brain and, sure enough, George's ability to understand and use language was impaired. With help from therapy and the natural recovery of his brain, George's language improved so much that, by the age of six-and-a-half, his language no longer presented a major problem.

As his language improved, however, it became increasingly apparent that his pronunciation and voice had also been affected. He could not easily sustain voice for a full sentence and his pronunciation was very slightly slurred. George's brain lesion had extended beyond areas which dealt specifically with language.

OPPORTUNITIES FOR LANGUAGE LEARNING

Babies with physical disabilities do not have the same control over themselves or their immediate world as those who are fully able. Even feeding, so essential for bonding between mother and child, is fraught with difficulties. They miss much of what is commonplace in the everyday life experience of other children. As we know, a great deal of learning takes place before baby gets as far as producing anything speech-like. Babies are communicating long before they produce 'real' words. These pre-verbal skills are the foundation stones upon which the child will build his speech and language abilities.

Just as significant, however, is the important role of feeding. Establishing the skills necessary for eating and drinking are as important to speech and communication development as rolling, sitting up and crawling are to standing up and walking. Difficulties with one of these invariably precede difficulties with skills which come later.

We have to ask ourselves, when do we stop during the day to relax and consciously communicate with others? The answer must surely be, when we eat. In fact, mealtimes provide a glorious opportunity to learn so many of the skills we need to take us through life. The whole atmosphere and regularity of mealtime encourages a child to develop feeding skills—sucking, swallowing, weaning, chewing, drinking— so that by the age of two they resemble those of an adult. Mealtimes also encourage early bonding between children and parents, and as the children grow they have the opportunity to practise a whole variety of social skills, such as turn-taking, discipline, the sharing of food and parents with others.

An expert colleague of mine stresses what a wonderful opportunity it is for language learning; so much vocabulary, associated with 'what's mine'—known as 'possession': 'my place, not yours'. With time: 'I am going to eat; am eating; have eaten; all gone; finished!' Mealtimes are where a child meets people outside the family, at birthdays, Christmas and so on. Mealtimes play a central role in establishing family relationships, where the protocols of acceptable social behaviour are learned.

Feeding Difficulties
Disability interferes with so many aspects of feeding. Abnormal muscle tone, either stiffness or floppiness, creates difficulties with placing the child in the right position and often muscles associated directly with feeding are affected, leading to poor movement, co-ordination and function. Equally, any structural abnormalities such as cleft lip or palate are likely to cause problems.

Children with physical disability frequently suffer from a wider range of medical problems than normal children. These can affect feeding, and some of them may be the result of as well as the cause of, feeding difficulties—for example, food going down 'the wrong way' and finding its way into a lung, resulting in a particularly nasty form of pneumonia.

Another problem, which would not necessarily be easily apparent to the lay person, is that of 'sensitivity'—not the kind which affects feelings, but the type that affects movement. All of us are born with what are called reflexes. One of the best known is the 'startle' reflex, whereby the baby's arms go up and back in a distinctive and recognisable fashion. As we mature, which means our neurological system matures, we learn to inhibit these reflexes. There are such reflexes associated with feeding, the most obvious being sucking and swallowing, and one we are all familiar with, the 'gag' reflex. Others exist, which are triggered at the wrong time by the presence in a child's mouth of food or feeding utensils.

Some children cannot tolerate being touched, especially near or around their mouths, let alone having anything inside them. It is hardly surprising, then, that for such children the whole idea of food and anything associated becomes repulsive. The chances are that somewhere, and at some time, they have had a bad experience, particularly if they are completely reliant on being fed by someone else. Put yourself in their shoes: imagine having food pushed into your mouth when you don't want it or like it, even before you've managed to swallow the previous mouthful. If feeding is so difficult, then the whole prospect of mealtimes can become a nightmare. No wonder it can at times become a fraught experience for the child, its parents, in fact everyone. It is not the motivating, enjoyable, social and supportive time experienced by able-bodied children, surrounded by their parents and friends.

Those early, non-verbal means of communicating—facial expression, gesture, body position, posture, and early speechlike sounds of gurgling, cooing and so on—which form a large part of the basic foundation of language, are often severely affected by physical disability. Think about it for a moment. Not easy, is it, to show how you feel if you cannot control the muscles of your face, when maybe a grimace is consistently interpreted as a smile—especially when perhaps you are feeling awful.

It is very difficult for children who have physical disabilities to organise and co-ordinate themselves, to express their feelings. Sometimes muscles controlling speech are so severely affected that absolutely no sounds can be made. Imagine the intense frustration experienced by children who have these difficulties. How do you learn about things in the world, what they are for, how they work, their relevance to you and others, if you cannot play with them, have experiences, in the normal way? Think, for example, how young babies put things in their mouths, and of the complex sequence of movements to be executed to do that, let alone how much is learned by doing it. If your body does not work, how do you learn about what it can do? How do you relate to the rest of the world? Children need to be 'active' learners to be in charge of themselves and their surroundings. In this way they learn quickly and efficiently. They are highly motivated, because the desire, the will and the initiative come from within.

The Importance of Other People

We learn about other people through our contact with them. This contact can be affected if the children's approaches and replies are not always made at the right time. They are frequently met by incomprehension, rejection, and sometimes they are even ignored. Babies use people rather like tools, to be manipulated, in order to learn about the world and what it contains. Remember that wonderful game all babies play, of throwing a toy on the floor, time after time, then waiting for it to be retrieved.

Situations such as this contain potential for a child acquiring the skills of language and communication. It's not too difficult to see how easily the child who is physically disabled can experience difficulty in learning, how fragmented and incomplete his knowledge is likely to be. Even everyday sounds may not have meaning. This is due to the problems children who are physically disabled encounter locating sounds, and making sense of them. Consider how difficult it is to attribute the ticking sound you hear to a clock, if you are unable to locate the source. How much greater, then, the difficulty of learning language, if a child has damage to the area of the brain concerned with language learning, or if he learns slowly, owing to the diffuse damage to his brain?

HOW SPEECH AND LANGUAGE THERAPISTS CAN HELP

Any child with physical disability is likely to have more than one handicapping condition; his needs, both in the short and long term, are therefore likely to be complex. A team approach to both assessment and management is crucial, and inevitably a wide range of professionals is involved, not all at the same time. The active help of a colleague from another profession is needed for both assessment and therapy. For example, it is extremely difficult for the speech and language therapist even to begin finding out what a child can understand or say, unless that child has been properly positioned by the physiotherapist. Each professional can also be observing the child from his or her own particular perspective whilst another is working.

Working together also has the added benefit of efficiency, for children with complex disabilities often tire rapidly, are easily distracted and, if only one professional at a time is involved, may need to be seen on more than one occasion. Naturally, this is a waste of time and energy. What is needed is a philosophy in which a well-planned and co-ordinated system is in place, which is of benefit to the child.

Perhaps more so than with any other group, the assessment and management of children with such complex disabilities involves many factors—the consideration of the child, his needs and that of his family. What therapy, treatment, and equipment will he need? What sort of education will be required and where will he be educated? How best to support his and his family's emotional and social needs? And how will the family be able to cope with him physically, and with the practical problems of every day family survival? These and many other issues need to be taken into consideration, which most likely would not have so much significance for children with other types of speech and language disability.

David had spastic quadriplegia. His physical disability was severe—so severe, in fact, that it had not been possible, during home visits, to assess all his needs. Obviously, something had to be organised to enable David to receive appropriate treatment, so it was arranged for him to attend a specialist centre for an assessment, where all who could help him were under one roof. Previously, in his home town, he had been bounced around like a ping-pong ball, from one profession to another, without any progress being made to solve his problems. A co-ordinated approach was needed, to assess his true potential and alleviate the deformities which had developed as a result of his physical disability. David and his family spent four complete days with various members of the team at a Regional Assessment Centre, as shown in Figure 12.

At the conclusion of the assessment period, a case conference, held to discuss David's future, made a full statement of his needs. The Local Education Authority, responsible for making decisions as to how and where these recommendations could best be met, decided that David should attend the centre where children with physical disability had access to both hospital and educational facilities. It was felt that his medical problems could not easily be managed within a local school. Surgery was needed, which would be spread out over several years; then there was the matter of his education: unless he could be taught in hospital he would be missing vital schooling.

David stayed at the centre for the next four years, during which time his deformities were dealt with and he received

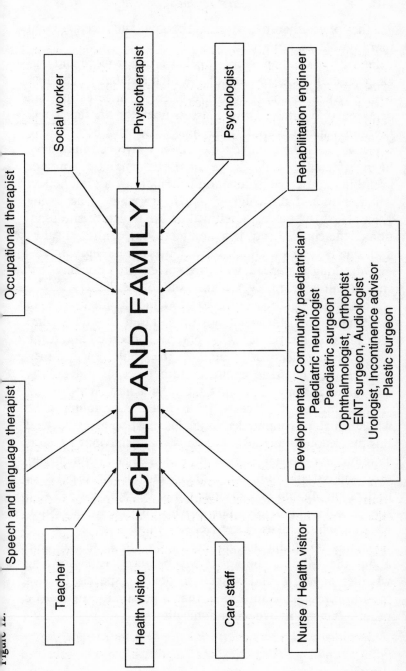

Figure 12.

Teacher

Speech and language therapist

Occupational therapist

Social worker

Physiotherapist

Psychologist

Rehabilitation engineer

Health visitor

Care staff

Nurse / Health visitor

CHILD AND FAMILY

Developmental / Community paediatrician
Paediatric neurologist
Paediatric surgeon
Ophthalmologist, Orthoptist
ENT surgeon, Audiologist
Urologist, Incontinence advisor
Plastic surgeon

Reproduced by courtesy of Chailey Heritage Rehabilitation and Development Centre.

all the physiotherapy, speech therapy and occupational
therapy that he required.

Perhaps more than with any other group, speech and language therapists are aware of the high number of children
with physical disability who are likely to have eating and
drinking difficulties. During assessment the therapist will
therefore spend considerable time observing how and in
what ways all the complex movements involved may have
been affected. At the same time she will also consider
breathing and voice production (phonation), asking herself
whether or not the child is actually capable of achieving
voice. Next to be considered will be the structure and function of the child's head, face and teeth, the control of saliva
and, finally, reflexes and posture. Unless problems with eating, drinking and swallowing are solved, it is unlikely that
speech will develop, even if the potential is there.

Sometimes parents are amazed at the detailed work an
assessment entails, especially with children who have complex physical disabilities. One parent, concerned about the
length of time needed to complete the whole range of procedures, was heard to comment rather despairingly, 'Why
is it taking so long? She can't talk, that's all that's wrong.'

What has taken place so far is just the beginning. The
whole range of communication skills must be assessed, and
this means observing all that non-verbal behaviour which is
so important—facial expression, eye gaze and contact, gesture and vocalisation. Then there are all the aspects of
understanding and use of language to be looked at, as well
speech skills. It is a potentially exhausting time for any child,
which is why it takes place over several days.

At this point, having gathered a wealth of information
about the child, a therapist may be faced with deciding
whether or not a child is likely to develop speech, at least
for the foreseeable future. Is that a possibility, or will he
require 'augmentative' communication?

Augmentative Systems of Communication

You may be wondering why the term 'augmentative' is used rather than 'alternative', since most people seeing a child with some other form of communication immediately assume that he is mute. This is far from the truth: most children can achieve some minimal speech and it is most important that at all times they are encouraged to use this to accompany the system, no matter how limited it may be. Any system should be seen as an additional, rather than an 'instead of' means of communication. Many types of non-verbal communication system are available, and are being used by children with severe speech impairment.

Nowadays, with the exciting developments in information technology, speech synthesisers are becoming increasingly available for children who are likely to find speech particularly difficult. A word of caution, though: these devices do not always come up to everyone's expectations, especially those of the user; speech can sound quite robotic, and it is frequently difficult to understand. Also, as with all technology, they are often only as useful as the skill of the user allows. For those children whose language is poor, we often find that other, simpler methods of non-speech communication are more appropriate. So let us examine what other augmentative systems are available to teach a child language and at the same time enable him to become a more efficient communicator.

Signing Systems

Signing is certainly one possibility. However, you must realise that even the simplest of the signing systems assumes a fair degree of hand control. Nevertheless, since the degree to which children are physically impaired varies widely, many are able to sign. We are fortunate to have such a wide range of choice.

British Sign Language (BSL) is the system used by the Deaf population in Britain. As it has evolved from natural gesture, it is most expressive; deaf people use not only their hands to express themselves, but also their bodies and facial expressions. Interestingly, it does not follow the grammar or word order of spoken language; instead, it has its own. Rather like a foreign language, it can be difficult for the hearing population to learn and understand. For example, instead of the sentence, 'A dark, handsome man rides and walks,' it would be signed, 'Man—dark—handsome—walk—ride.'

One of the more commonly used systems is the *Makaton Vocabulary*, which was developed in the 1970s for use by deaf adults with severe learning difficulties. It uses selected signs from BSL, those considered most useful in providing basic communication. Due to its simplicity, the easy, large, hand movements and the fact that key words are signed following the patterns of development of speech, it has proved to be very useful with young children.

Signed English is a relatively recent innovation. Again, signs from BSL are used. The system follows the order of spoken language, but with added signs, called 'markers', to indicate grammatical features. Again, simplicity is one of its great advantages.

Sir Richard Paget originally experimented with the idea of forming a universal sign language, a kind of visual Esperanto, based initially upon the use of Ogden's Basic English. During his lifetime the focus of his work gradually changed, and after his death was continued by Dr Pierre Gorman and Lady Paget, who formed the *Paget–Gorman* signing system, for use by the deaf population. Unlike BSL, it is not based on natural gesture but on American Indian signs, which might at first seem a strange source but in fact is quite logical. With something like sixty-five different languages to contend with, the North American Indians devised a mutual set of hand signs, in which each group of ideas has its own sign and is further elaborated by additional gesture—for example, 'animal' with one hand and an additional gesture using the other hand for, say, 'horse'.

The Paget–Gorman signing system has a vocabulary of

4,000 signs and all aspects of English grammar can be signed. For children with physical impairment it is not always a first choice, since it requires a high degree of hand control. There are other systems available, but because they require a great deal of manual dexterity, they are not very useful for children who are physically disabled.

Symbol Systems

Manual systems are only one of the ways in which children with physical disability can communicate. The other major means of augmentative communication, of great benefit to children who have little voluntary movement as well as little or no speech, is by the use of various types of symbols. Remember, a symbol is representative of something else. We see them all about us: road signs and letters are visual symbols. Then there are sirens which are auditory symbols. Symbol systems, ranging from the very simple to the complex and abstract, have been developed for teaching language, and a means of communication, to children with physical impairment.

The Makaton Vocabulary (the signing system) has a set of symbols, based on its vocabulary, which can if necessary be used in conjunction with the manual signs. There are other very simple symbols called 'rebuses', which are line drawings representative of objects, actions and attributes. An 'attribute' tells us something about an object—for example, its size, shape or colour and, if it was a human being, an attribute would be how we feel.

As these symbols are so simple, once a child's language has begun to develop, a more complex and abstract system called *Blissymbols* is often introduced. These symbols look like the things they represent; they also represent ideas, so that even though each sign has a word written above it, the meaning would not be restricted to that single word. In the long term, of course, the words help a child to read. So symbol systems are frequently used as a short-term measure, until a child with very poor speech becomes more intelligible, or until one who is more severely impaired moves on to using written language.

As you can imagine, for children who have not previously had a coherent means of communication, signing and symbols are liberating. Jo had complex and severe physical disabilities which had previously interfered with all attempts to provide him with a means of communication. Following an assessment at a specialist centre where he had received treatment, his life had changed for the better; moreover, his therapist had successfully introduced him to symbols.

Much to her surprise, Jo's progress was exceptional. Because he had begun learning rather late in his short life, there was a sense of urgency about teaching him as much as possible as quickly as possible, and it was at this point that he rebelled. On the fateful day, as usual his therapist wanted to know what he had been doing and told him what she had planned for the session. Using his Blissymbols Jo told her to 'go away, I don't want to talk to you today.' Astonished, she asked him why. 'Because I don't feel like it,' he replied. It was a wonderful turning point in Jo's therapy: for the first time in his life he had been able to say that he did not want to do something, just like any other child!

Many youngsters with little or no speech have had their lives changed through being able to use all kinds of electronic communication aids, which can be adapted for use with symbol systems. Although computer technology has made a major contribution, sometimes the amount of time it takes for the user to manipulate the technology can be so frustrating, that it is often quicker to use the tried and tested communication board. No doubt, as technology improves, all this will change.

You may well be wondering how we know which, of all the communication aids available, would be best for a particular child. We are fortunate in Britain to have a network of communication aids centres and assessment centres, which provide a unique opportunity for the most appropriate aid to be recommended.

Like everyone else, children frequently use a variety of ways to communicate; sometimes, as with Sally, who had severe athetosis, the few sounds they can produce are a completely inadequate means of expressing themselves. Before anything could be done about assessing Sally's communication skills, she had required advice from the physiotherapists and rehabilitation engineer, in order to find the right chair, support and position to give her maximum voluntary movement. A rehabilitation engineer researches, designs and builds all types of aids to promote rehabilitation—arms, chairs, computer communication systems and so on.

At this point the speech therapist, in consultation with her colleagues, had found that Sally could 'eye point'. This means looking at an object or person to identify them, rather than physically pointing; we all do it all the time without realising it, but for children with physical disability it is a skill that can be developed in order to communicate. Sally was also at a stage in her language learning when she was ready to learn symbols.

She was introduced to Blissymbols and taught how to point to what she wanted to say, using her eyes; at the same time she began learning the words associated with the symbols. This was a great breakthrough which made a huge difference to her life, but there was another problem which caused her some discomfort. Sally dribbled rather excessively, which she disliked and wanted to control, for, to her dismay, it also caused extra work for everyone else.

With the help of the therapist she was taught how to maintain better lip closure, and given a small bleeper to wear, which reminded her to swallow every few minutes. Soon, she had begun to swallow without reminders and so was able to control the worst of her dribbling. As her skill at using Blissymbols improved, she needed a faster method of accessing them, so colour was introduced as a way of classifying them. All Sally then had to do was look at a part of the board on which a small template of colours was located.

Whoever was with her immediately knew at which group of symbols she would be looking. From then on, Sally carried a communication board around with her, on her wheelchair; this gave her a wonderful feeling of independence. Most important of all, as far as she was concerned, she could now talk to anyone she wanted to.

EDUCATION

Understandably, one of the great worries of any parent is how and where their child who has a physical disability will be educated. Parents do have a choice, but they can only make a decision when they have a full understanding of their child's disabilities. It is therefore the responsibility of the professionals to take time to explain the difficulties, in terms that can be understood, in order for the best decisions to be made about the child's education. I well recall a consultant explaining to parents about their child's condition and using the term 'morbidity'. From the horrified looks on their faces, I knew they had interpreted it as meaning that their child would die, which of course was far from the truth.

It would be rather dogmatic to say that there are basically two options for a child's education, either mainstream or special school, because this is not always the case. There are many authorities who have most imaginative schemes allowing children to attend both—each for part of the week. Some parents prefer their child to attend a special school, with all its advantages of specialist facilities, therapy and teaching. Others, on the other hand, want the experiences for their children, of people and everyday life, that only a mainstream school can offer.

Access to a full multidisciplinary team is usually only available at what is known as a Regional Assessment Centre. Such centres provide an assessment service to authorities within that region, whilst some of them also care for and educate a number of children whose complex disabilities require the continuing help of most members of the team.

Some education authorities have their own schools for physically disabled children, whilst others choose to use the facilities provided by a private school run by one of the charities, like the Spastics Society.

Regular reviews of a child's progress enable us to provide the most appropriate treatment or education. What is right for your child at age six may be totally inappropriate at age eleven, and no doubt you will want the most suitable school or therapy, even though this will mean change; flexibility and patience are required by everyone.

A final word on the argument between those who subscribe fervently to the Peto Method of Conductive Education and those who, over the years, have used all the other tried and tested methods found to be most effective. Unfairly, I believe, there has been a great deal of criticism of those who question the claims of the Peto method and suggest that it is not the answer to every child's difficulties.

In Hungary, where the method was developed, children thought to be suitable are selected at an early age, and undoubtedly they will benefit from the method because they have been identified as having the potential to do so. Peto's philosophy of having a key person, the conductor, through which all aspects of work, enthusiasm and effort are channelled, does have much to commend it. The children are made responsible for their own movement, in order to get around and do everyday activities. We know from research how children, as active learners, show greater enthusiasm to learn and progress rapidly to becoming independent learners.

It is unfortunate that, instead of promoting Conductive Education as yet another, but welcome method of treatment, media attention has portrayed it as the miracle cure. Years of research support the effectiveness of methods currently in use, and to infer that these, and the people who subscribe to them, are failing, is far from the truth. It is hardly surprising that highly experienced physiotherapists, occupational therapists and speech and language therapists feel somewhat indignant, since they have only asked questions about its claims. Conductive Education has been shown to be most effective with certain children, but research is required in order to identify, early in their lives, those children who will benefit from this approach to treatment. Without research, it is difficult to make informed decisions about all the types of treatment needed by the children in our care.

7 Autism

> My greatest anxiety at first was that Anthony did not speak. His other problems seemed to pale into insignificance, to take second place, to this over-riding fact—he just couldn't speak. It is only now, when he can actually speak so well, that my anxiety is concentrated on his bizarre—it's the only way to describe it—his bizarre behaviour.

Anthony's mum only gradually began to realise that her son had more than just a language problem; the rather odd behaviour she had noticed early in his life she had attributed to his inability to speak. Both she and her husband had noticed his obsession with anything that revolved, for he would twirl or spin anything that moved. The family ran a washeteria business and were greatly concerned lest his early exposure to circulating washing-machine drums had been the cause of his 'obsession'.

Anthony showed little or no emotion, no matter how dreadful the act he had just committed—whether it was the daily destruction of toys or hitting another child. There were other oddities in his behaviour pattern—for example, his play consisted of lining up cars and endlessly spinning their wheels—but it was his lack of affection for themselves and his brother which so distressed and bewildered them.

Anthony's eye contact was unusual: he would fix his gaze and never let it waver, and although he did not always focus accurately, this concentrated gaze understandably caused the recipient a great deal of discomfort. He frequently hurt other children with apparently little conception of why they were making such a fuss. Failure to develop language was just one part of the total picture, for in fact Anthony was suffering from a hidden and yet crippling impairment—that of autism.

As speech and language therapists, we are often involved with the family at an early stage in their autistic child's development, since poor language is one of the impairments associated with autism, and of course its lack of development causes great concern. Autism, however, is far more than just an inability to communicate; all the problems described by Anthony's mum are aspects of what researchers in the field of autism refer to as a 'triad of impairments', a complex phrase which really means three impairments, all concerned with social interaction. The three aspects of the triad are:

— An impairment of social recognition or relationships.

— An impairment of social communication.

— An impairment of social understanding and imagination.

Even for the professional, autism is difficult to define; it is both complex and diverse. For example, individuals with the most extreme form of impairment of social relationships appear totally aloof and indifferent to other people, whilst less impaired individuals may be more approachable but will not necessarily make any contact themselves. Those who are least impaired may superficially appear to be normal, but their lack of true understanding of the subtleties of social rules and perceptiveness of others very quickly becomes apparent.

Impairment of social communication, in its most extreme form, is shown often by a total absence of the wish or desire to communicate with others. Less impaired individuals may make literal comments, often irrelevant to the conversation, whilst those least impaired may talk a great deal, irrespective of the wishes or responses of their listeners, and have a monologue rather than a conversation.

With those most severely affected in the impairment of social understanding and imagination, any form of copying or pretend play is totally absent and those less impaired may have no spontaneous pretend play, but are able to copy the actions of others without any true understanding of their purpose or meaning. The sort of repetitive and ritualistic play you frequently see, such as endlessly pushing the toy train round the track, can in no way be considered true play. More able, less severely affected individuals may be able to recognise other people's feelings, but again, these are learnt rather than being based on true misunderstanding.

The puzzling question of why autism can appear to be so diverse can most easily be explained by using the analogy of a spectrum. Remember your schooldays when you looked at colours? No doubt, your teacher showed you how colours start at the white end of the spectrum and gradually fade into each other until you reach the darker colours. Autism can be thought of in the same way, encompassing dramatically different degrees of severity—varying from profound handicap in some children, through to the more subtle problems of social understanding seen in individuals of apparently average or above average ability.

The Pioneers
Before going further, I must say something about the early pioneers of autism, because sooner or later you will hear them referred to, most likely in terms such as 'classic Kanner autism' or 'Asperger's syndrome'.

More than 50 years ago, Leo Kanner in the United States first published an account of autism, and he was closely followed by Hans Asperger in Germany. Both gave detailed descriptions of the disorder, attempting at the same time to provide a theory to explain it. Independently both had seen cases of rather strange children who had in common similar odd features in their behaviour.

Because of the Second World War, Asperger's work is not widely known, and Kanner is usually credited with being the first to recognise and describe the disorder. His description of a number of features was perceived as representing the classic syndrome, but over the years it has become apparent that not all children have all these features present in their autistic behaviour.

Asperger's description of the children he observed contained some of the features described by Kanner, and researchers now suggest that both Kanner and Asperger were describing autistic children, Kanner referring to those who are less able, with extreme impairments, and Asperger to those who are more able. Kanner's work has become the most quoted in the field of autism and yet, in fact, Asperger was describing the same condition. What in recent years has become known as Asperger's syndrome is a convenient and useful label reserved for the rather rare, very able and verbal autistic child.

Kanner is credited with producing an extensive list of features, which vividly described the so-called classic features of autism. Yet despite all of these he was convinced that only two were of what he called cardinal significance, the first of which he identified as 'autistic aloneness'. Through his keen observation he identified the outstanding, in-built and fundamental problem of the children—the inability to relate in the ordinary way to people and situations, right from the beginning of life. It is interesting that Asperger also referred to this aspect of autistic behaviour, by observing that autistic children were never on the same wavelength as other normal children with whom they had contact. This extreme autistic aloneness is there from the beginning.

The second feature, again recognised by both researchers, was the autistic child's obsessive desire for sameness: the monotonous repetitions of actions, words and thoughts, the elaborate routines and the choice of one topic to the exclusion of all others. Some of the children showed outstanding ability with specific aspects of learning, which impressed both researchers, and although rather puzzled by this, they believed these were indications of good intelligence. Kanner and Asperger were both of the opinion that the cause of autism was a problem with which children are born, a belief supported by the researchers of today. So much for the background.

THEORIES OF AUTISM

What causes autism has perplexed researchers ever since Kanner and Asperger first described it. Current thinking, as I have said, is that autism is innate—in other words, it is ultimately caused by some biological fault, presumably apparent well before birth. It would not be unreasonable to suppose, depending on the sort and extent of the damage, that autism might be considered a 'pure' disorder, but it can also occur together with other impairments. This might go some way to explaining the puzzle of why autistic children can vary so much: some develop into what are very odd but articulate people, whilst others never even learn to speak.

Not so long ago, a fashionable theory was circulating that poor parenting was the cause of autism. Although we know now that this is a myth, at the time it caused much anguish for many parents. For this to have been credible, it would have been necessary for all the children in the family to be suffering from autism and this patently was not the case.

Current research indicates that autism is associated with a wide range of neurological conditions and should be regarded in the same way as cerebral palsy—in other words, that a variety of conditions causes disturbed development of the brain. This is apparent in the high number of children who have varying degrees of learning difficulty (still referred to sometimes as mental handicap)—approximately three quarters of all autistic children. With families who already have an autistic child, research has also shown that there is an increased risk (something like one in six) of having another child who, although not autistic, will have certain kinds of learning difficulty, including language disorder, poor organisation of body movements and sometimes poor social skills.

Three to four children in every 10,000 have classic autism, like that described by Kanner. Approximately twenty in every 10,000 have closely related conditions—those who show fewer of the features of autism. As with other disabling conditions, statistics indicate that far more boys than girls are affected; in the case of autism the ratio is four boys to one girl and in most cases the onset of autism is apparent by the age of three.

How to Explain Autistic Behaviour

The enigma of autism continues to challenge both those who work with individuals who have autism, and those who are devoted to research. Is it an emotional disorder, a cognitive disorder or one of social understanding? A recent theory suggests it is within the area of social understanding that the problem exists—to know that other people have minds and to understand how they think. Sooner or later, any adult who plays with young children will enter into their world of make-believe, of shared pretence. Remember your two-year-old who pours out a pretend cup of tea from a toy teapot and then, with a wicked but knowing smile, empties it over your head? You are then expected to be wet and horrified at what has been done, and to mop it up. Your child, without yet realising it, is becoming aware that you have a mind. This early shared pretence is the first indication of what is called a 'theory of mind', the conscious knowledge of other people's thoughts, which develops between the ages of three and four.

Understanding how other people think enables us to perceive beyond the immediate and obvious, beyond the knowledge of what objects look and feel like, what they are called, to appreciating the differences between a banana and a telephone, a car and a horse. Pretence takes us to a different level of thinking and understanding—for a child to know, for example, that when mum playfully talks into a banana, it really represents a telephone.

This ability to read and understand other people's minds is totally lacking in autistic people, caused, it is suggested, by the faulty development of one component of the child's mind. This 'theory of mind' enables us to distinguish between 'really meaning it' and 'just pretending', or between telling a joke and a lie. This is something individuals who have autism cannot do.

Theory and the Three Core Impairments

The idea of problems with understanding how people think does seem to make sense in relation to the three 'core' impairments of autism. You will recall the first was about social relationships. How are we able to make and sustain such subtle and sophisticated relationships? How can we judge, feel and actually know what others might be thinking without relying on obvious clues? For example, a smile can so easily not be a smile, but it takes a great deal of sophistication to know that. We all know, don't we, when someone is not really smiling? Something about their eyes, their face, their whole body language, betrays them.

And what about communication? If I am to understand and interpret what you really mean when you are talking—your true intentions—I really do have to have a fair idea of what is going on inside your head. Also, it is not only what you say, but the way that you say it. Recently, the speech therapist had been working with Sam, a very able older autistic child. His special needs teacher came in and asked the therapist how Sam had been behaving. 'Oh, he's been awful,' she said in a teasing voice and with a smile on her face. Poor Sam was distraught, totally missing the intention of what had been said, and interpreting it quite literally.

Pretend play, as I mentioned earlier, is a sure sign that a child perceives beyond the here and now, the literal; it indicates that he has knowledge of social understanding and imagination. Any observer in the playground sees the most amazing stories and games enacted, for children have this wonderful ability to transport themselves to anywhere, do anything, be anything. Poor Lee, an able autistic child in a mainstream school, desperately wanted to be friends with the other children and in turn they wanted to include him, well aware of his differences and most accepting of them. The problem always arose in the playground, when Lee was expected to be a dragon or Thomas the Tank Engine or some other make-believe creature. Complaints came fast and furious—'He won't try, he's spoiling our game, he's getting in the way'—but poor Lee was doing none of these. He really had no idea what it was all about. How could he possibly be anything other than a boy, because that was what he was? Quite simply, he did not know how to pretend. Pretence is a game we all play, adults as well as children. Remember how Walter Mitty, with all his pretence and imagination, conquered the world? How many times have you been the most beautiful, handsome, clever, articulate person, who does wonderful things? All in your imagination, of course!

WHAT IS AUTISTIC LANGUAGE?

More often than not, the most obvious problem causing most concern in young children later diagnosed as autistic is delayed language development, so speech therapists are among the first professionals to see these children. What is it, then, at this very early stage, which might give us an indication of autism as a diagnosis rather than some other cause?

If we accept that a theory of mind does not develop until the age of three to four years, we need to be aware of the early signs of the normal development of 'mind-reading'. In Chapter 2 I discussed the normal development of communication at a pre-linguistic level. Those early but vital links between mother and baby, what we call 'shared understanding'; those foundations which are laid in the first year of a child's life, which encompass such aspects of communication as joint attention, eye and finger pointing, the development of dialogue and turn-taking, social timing, and the understanding and use of pitch and intonation—it has aptly been described as a 'conversation without words'. Since it is these very aspects of communication which are frequently lacking in young children who are subsequently diagnosed as autistic, careful assessment and observation at an early stage in development may give us the clues to the diagnosis of autism.

Children Who are Mute

Although the diagnosis of autism does not necessarily mean a child won't be able to master the actual mechanics of learning to speak, a large number of children who have autism never speak at all or have very severely delayed language. One possible reason for this may be the high incidence of severe learning difficulty in this group of children. Even to begin to speak, children need to reach a particular stage in their general development. So, for example, if the child does not even attain the age of eighteen months in his development, then it is highly unlikely that he will ever learn to speak.

Of course there are always children who do not have such severe learning difficulties and yet still remain mute; we read about them in the literature or occasionally see them mentioned in the media. These children, although fairly unusual, show abilities elsewhere, which suggest that they are intelligent enough to speak. One such child produced the most amazing, beautifully detailed drawings of buildings, and another was so gifted mathematically, he was able to deal with numbers at incredible speed. So far we do not know why these children remain mute but, no doubt, given time, an answer will be found.

Speaking is only one way of communicating. Some autistic children, although mute, do learn to communicate through other means, usually manual signing. It is not unusual, however, for them, or for children with severely delayed language, to have problems with signing, because gesture as a means of communication is not meaningful to them. Theirs is a total communication failure. They show very little desire to communicate and, more than likely, their social relationships would be very poor. This leads us to believe that their autism is particularly severe.

The Two-Way Channel

Babies, as we know, within the first year of life learn about the give and take of human communication; but for children and adults with autism, such two-way interaction is a source of great difficulty—in fact one of the early signs of autism is the child's lack of response to speech. Regardless of the language, being called by your name evokes a tremendous response and is a very powerful reason for wanting to communicate. To be addressed in this way carries with it a sort of guarantee that whatever follows is going to be of importance, especially for you.

We all learn how to be successful communicators, building on those skills learned without conscious thought, so early in life. We know how to pause and hand over to the other person, when to interrupt and take over, how to pick up the subtle signals from the listener that it's his turn to speak; how, in fact, to do all this without appearing rude. Autistic people find this very difficult, frequently appearing rude or embarrassing, overbearing, not knowing when to stop.

As normal communicators we are usually concerned to get over our point of view in the most efficient and persuasive way possible. Take too long and you've lost your listener; be too brief and you fail to make your point. This incredible communication tight-rope, which we walk along all the time, is not one that is understood by autistic people.

The Echo

Nothing is more disconcerting than having everything you say repeated verbatim, especially when you are attempting to have a conversation, however simple. Some parents find this lack of spontaneous speech quite wearing, but it is not limited to this alone. The echo can be delayed and, just when you think you've made your point, your whole utterance is repeated, rather as if there is a time delay. The child who has autism most often makes use of a few stock phrases, many repetitions and very few topics, and for even the most caring parents, who may have been relieved to hear speech and language developing, it can all prove to be extraordinarily irritating.

What they want to hear is the right speech at the right moment. To hear 'kiss me' repeated twenty times is enough to provoke a rather different response from the one requested. One mother whose child spoke non-stop described him as a 'chatterbox from a different planet, going nowhere with nobody'. All she wanted, she said, was for him to stop occasionally and, just at the right moment, acknowledge her or his father with a smile.

This kind of echoing, repetitive speech has very little value in terms of actual communication. Just listen to children developing language in the normal way, who can utter one word and with it convey so much. From the way autistic children use language, which is distinctively different from able children, it is possible to speculate that perhaps they do not learn it in quite the same way. We appear to be born with the ability to learn rules about language and, from our understanding of these, we can formulate an infinite and varied number of sentences. Lizzie, who has autism, whilst playing with a toy teddy said:

'I saw a teddy' (repeated about five times).
'I saw a teddy sleep in the bed.'
'I saw a teddy sleep in the car.'
'I saw a teddy sleep on the chair.'

Repetitive speech, in fact repetitive behaviour of all kinds, has yet to be explained and understood. Certainly, repeating learnt phrases at the wrong moment can have embarrassing results.

Robert had entered a language unit, as a child with very little understanding or use of language and some rather odd social skills, but not until he acquired language, which happened quite rapidly, did the staff realise he had a number of problems, apart from his language difficulties. He had only a few topics of conversation, his eye contact was poor, and much of the time he was in his own world, but there were occasions when he appeared relatively coherent.

When the school was due to have a visit from the inspectorate, Robert's teacher realised she had a fundamental problem. How could she explain his difficulties, when for periods of time he appeared perfectly coherent? Regardless, she made a creditable attempt at an explanation, but it was apparent the inspector was puzzled, since Robert was doing his maths, at which he was quite gifted, and answering questions with obvious ease. Any doubts, however, were swiftly dispelled when, out of the blue, while not looking at the inspector, Robert said, 'And do you snog with your wife in bed?' and then continued his maths as if nothing had happened! His poor teacher was not quite sure whether to laugh or cry, even though Robert had admirably demonstrated his difficulties.

Peter, on the other hand, had his own pet phrases which he used every day and no one, including his parents, knew where or how these originated. They were used frequently, which was a sure sign of communication failure, since the listener had no idea what they referred to, and Peter made no attempt to explain why he had said them. If you or I decide to say something totally irrelevant, for whatever reason, we will always follow it up by some remark or explanation, in order that others will not consider us to be ridiculous.

How You Say Things is Important
The way in which our voices go up and down in pitch, the way we stress certain words or parts of words, the quality of our voice, the rate at which we speak, all carry immeasurable meaning in what we are saying.

Reflect for a moment on how we convey sarcasm or irony, and you will begin to realise that it is far more than just the words we use, but more often the way in which we speak. In fact the way we say a phrase or sentence can mean the exact opposite of the words themselves: for example, 'Oh, on time today,' is instantly understood, if said in such a way, to mean 'late again!' Our language is full of such nuances. These finer meanings, both subtle and sophisticated, are the ones which autistic children and adults do not understand.

Autistic children's speech is noted for its odd and unusual intonation: it can sound flat and uninteresting, with the wrong emphasis, too loud, too soft, too fast or too slow. Other children, with speech and language problems of a different nature, also have difficulties with these aspects of language, and yet their speech is not recognised as being so distinctively different.

Words, Sentences, and Their Meaning
Those autistic children who do acquire language understand and use it in an extremely literal and concrete way and they learn words in a very patchy, selective fashion. They can have a stunning vocabulary when they are discussing their current obsession, whilst other words, expressing feelings and inner mental states, are not easily learned or understood. We are aware that meaning is not just how we understand single words, it is the combination of words together in sentences and the meaning that the whole unit conveys to us. We do not need to understand the meaning of every single word in a sentence, or even in a piece of prose, to understand the meaning of the whole. The saying, 'The whole is more than the sum of the parts', really does apply to our language. One researcher quoted the wonderful example, ''Twas brillig and the slithy toves did gyre and gimble in the wabe', and we know the feeling, the meaning, exactly, even though in terms of simple words it is utter nonsense. How we do this is as amazing as it is mysterious,

yet we do it all the time; but to autistic children this would be totally meaningless.

Some interesting research has been carried out to ascertain how easy it would be for both able and autistic children to recall sequences of meaningful as opposed to meaningless strings of words. For able children there is a desire to make sense and meaning out of strings of words; asking them to recall sequences of non-meaningful words is particularly difficult. For autistic children this makes little difference because, for them, the fact that something has meaning does not enhance their ability to remember.

The more complex and subtle language becomes, for example with discourse, narrative, repartee and jokes, the harder it becomes for autistic people, young and old, to understand. For those autistic children who do develop language, learning the rules of grammar and pronunciation presents few problems. Perhaps this is because these are governed by rules which are fairly logical and therefore do not have the same complications associated with understanding meaning. There is, however, one exception to this with many children and that is with the distinction between 'you' and 'I'. Unfortunately, these two words have a shifting meaning in conversation, because both listener and speaker can be 'you' and 'I' at the same time; it is hardly surprising, therefore, that children who have autism become confused, since the words refer to both people. In fact pronouns as a class of words present difficulties, because they always refer to something or somebody that has already been mentioned.

How Children With Autism Communicate Non-Verbally
Able or not, it is now recognised how lacking individuals with autism are in their natural gesture, facial expression and body language, for it is not only lacking but odd, and we recognise it as such. Children with autism do show signs of attachment. They are able to make approaches by touching and looking; they also respond to and use gesture indicating 'go away' or 'come here', but what are lacking are the

more expressive gestures, such as hiding one's face in embarrassment. What, then, is the difference between these two kinds of gestures? Well, the first kind are purely to influence people to make changes, somewhat like turning the radio on and off; whilst the second are the response you make when you realise what other people must be thinking or feeling about you.

Expressive gestures carry a wealth of meaning. The fractionally raised eyebrow can indicate so much: 'You and I both know that is not true.' Our communication with each other is littered with such hints, which powerfully govern our behaviour. It is this aspect of communication that autistic children and autistic adults fail to comprehend.

Who Makes a Diagnosis of Autism?
Because of the complex nature of autism, the actual diagnosis of the condition is not always easy or clear-cut. Since they are often the first profession to work with autistic children, speech therapists may well suspect that this is the underlying cause of a speech and language problem; however, they would always want to obtain the advice of other professionals.

The responsibility for telling parents is usually undertaken by the consultant in the team of professionals who have been working with the child. Most parents are naturally relieved when they know what is wrong with their child, but are often devastated when they receive the information. One mother said she had gone to see the consultant with a child who couldn't talk, and came away with a child who had a life sentence—that of autism. Perhaps, if she had immediately been given the opportunity to talk to other parents of autistic children, she might have felt far more positive about her child's condition: it is not necessarily a life sentence. She needed to understand that her child would change, learn, and achieve.

Against this despairing background, it is important for parents to have moral support in order to be able to come to terms with the diagnosis. Most of them would also appreciate the chance to make a return visit to see the consultant, in order to ask all those questions they could not think of, when they were told their child had autism.

EDUCATION

A child who has autism can be severely impaired and a non-communicator, or very able and very verbal. If you recall the spectrum of autism, children can fall anywhere in between these two extremes; therefore, what is suitable education for one would certainly not be for the other. Being autistic does not automatically mean attending a special school or placement; education authorities have become far more flexible in how they make provision, acknowledging that children with autism are not all the same, that they may require a variety of educational placements throughout their school lives.

Mainstream placement is the most frequent route to education for many of the more able autistic children, who will have a statement of need which could well recommend extra teaching support as well as an ancillary helper. Therapists work in a variety of ways with the staff who are working most closely with the child. Sometimes this will involve regular face-to-face contact with the child in school and liaison with staff, or alternatively, just advice and monitoring of the child's progress. Whatever programme of therapy we suggest will always need to be carried out as part of the child's daily routine, in order for it to be meaningful.

Flexibility
Some education authorities have taken a slightly different route to integrating autistic children, by providing classes or units attached to mainstream schools. In this way the children can benefit from the specialist teaching and therapy provided in the unit. At the same time they can gradually be introduced to working with other children, at a pace suitable to each individual child.

When unit facilities are not available, it may be that the child's needs are not totally met in a mainstream placement, and occasionally other arrangements can be made. Sally is a child who really requires far more structured teaching and therapy than is possible in a mainstream class. With her ancillary helper, she attends a special class for children with autism, which is attached to a local special school. Although somewhat disruptive to her school life, it does enable her to enjoy the best of both worlds—the contact with ordinary children, plus the specialist help she requires if she is to make progress.

Autistic children who have learning difficulties, those less able or more severely affected, may well attend a local MLD or SLD school. There they can receive the same kind of support as Sally, but on a full-time basis in order to deal with their complex problems.

The major difference between the child who is autistic and another child with severe learning difficulties is the autistic child's very uneven development. Whereas the very profoundly learning-disabled child would most likely be equally delayed in most areas of his development, the autistic child may have severely delayed social and communication skills, similar to or even less than a twelve-month-old baby, but in certain other learning skills be functioning much nearer his real age. Faced with this paradox, some MLD and SLD schools have established classes especially for autistic children, having found the teaching in mixed classes with both autistic and non-autistic children, not surprisingly, to be somewhat unsuccessful.

Special schools, purely for autistic children, are also an option, although many of these are privately run and Local Education Authorities will need to provide special funding for a child to attend. It is more than likely that the increasing demand on budgets may make this an unpopular choice. However, it is at these schools that there are highly specialist staff, small classes and that most important of commodities—time. It may be that this particular form of education

is the best for your child. If this is the case, you may well
need to be prepared to fight to get it!

How are Children with Autism Taught to Communicate?
Speech and language therapists are involved in the teaching
of communication skills from a very early stage in the autistic
child's development, and that therapy may continue in one
form or another throughout his school life. As I said earlier,
therapists work closely with all the professionals who are
involved with the child, and of course with the parents. It
must be said that just about every approach available has
been tried and tested with autistic children, from strict
behaviour modification to the more obscure, idiosyncratic
therapies, such as daily life therapy.

The modifying of certain kinds of behaviour, using reward
system, known as the 'behaviour approach', is used successfully in conjunction with other therapies. It is essential, as
far as is possible, to eliminate the unwanted obsessive movements—the spinning, hand-shaking, rocking, and so on—
in order for a child to learn effectively. This is needed to
encourage the early skills required for communication to
take place, as well as the development of spoken language.
Some parents find a deliberate reward system rather unacceptable, believing it to be a form of bribery, but if we
are scrupulously honest, we all use this with our children.
Can't we hear ourselves saying in desperation, 'David, if
you go and tidy your room, I'll let you watch *Neighbours*'?

Various studies have found that in the long term, when
this particular approach was used on its own, children did
not carry over what they had learned in 'the room' where
the therapy had taken place to situations elsewhere. As with
all therapies, there are claims and counterclaims for success.
Therapists, teachers and parents use what they know to be
successful for each individual child.

Other approaches are also used—for example, signing
systems based on BSL (British Sign Language), Paget–
Gorman and, in the United States, ASL (American Sign

Language). Experience and research indicate that the most useful sign language is one which is easy to learn, and most importantly includes features which follow the grammar of spoken language, as well as being widely used in the community to which the child with autism belongs. It is interesting that signs learned and used tend to be those which are concrete and easily change the behaviour of others, rather than those more abstract signs, which tend to express feelings or emotions.

Some children do not respond to either spoken or signed language, and with these even simpler forms of communication are used. These include plastic symbols, Blissymbols and pictures on communication boards. You can of course combine all these aids in a child's therapy programme, since none of them is mutually exclusive.

Most important of all with any approach is that it is meaningful in the child's life. If therapy does not relate in some way to the child's immediate surroundings and needs, he is less likely to be motivated or to perceive the need to use language as a means of communication.

Music in general, and music therapy in particular, is a wonderful medium through which children with learning difficulties can learn to communicate. It is particularly effective for autistic children in encouraging eye contact, turn-taking, social timing, correct rhythms for speech and, most of all, learning about shared understanding or the shared focus with which all conversations begin.

Holding therapy, used with other approaches, also encourages children, through the parents' insistence on comforting their child, to feel more secure and at the same time reduces premature independence. In the longer term, holding therapy aims to help improve relationships and therefore develop the most conducive atmosphere for reciprocal or shared understanding to take place.

The most recent therapy to come to the attention of therapists is called 'facilitated communication'. The technique was developed in Australia, and is now used widely in the United

States and Canada. It is a technique whereby someone called the 'facilitator' helps the person to type or point to a letterboard, by giving support to his hand, wrist or elbow, making it possible for him to choose letters. When the staff at the Geneva Centre in Toronto, Canada, tried an experiment a few years ago, with the help of five autistic children of widely varying ages and communicative ability, they were astonished at the language the children typed. The staff discovered that the children had taught themselves to read and spell and express themselves in full sentences.

The therapy has, of course, provoked controversy. It challenges fifty years of research, suggesting that if a child can produce written language of such discernment, then the assumptions we have all made about linguistic and social understanding are now turned upside down. So far, the claims made by facilitated communication have been greeted with anything from evangelical enthusiasm to cynical dismissal. Until we have the benefit of research to support those claims, I believe we have to keep an open mind.

There are many more approaches too numerous to list, including dietary regimes, psychotherapy, psychoanalysis, patterning treatments and various forms of medication. At the moment, regardless of the vast body of research undertaken, we know of no cure for autism and any such claims should be treated with caution. Prior to suggesting the most appropriate therapy or therapies for a child, we need to have a clear idea of his specific communication, social and learning problems; these can only be identified by careful assessment. All of us need to remind ourselves, professionals and parents alike, how children change as they mature, never forgetting that we must always be prepared to react to those changes.

8 Other Factors Affecting Speech and Language

So far I have concentrated on those communication diffi-culties and their causes which, over the years, have most concerned the parents with whom I have worked. Inevitably, the emphasis I have given is partly related to my own interests; however, there are certain other aspects of our work which I should mention. One of the obvious causes of speech and language impairment can be attributed to hearing loss. Traditionally, speech and language therapists have not been involved with the management of severe hearing impairment, but in the last few years this has changed.

You may wonder why visual impairment has been included in this chapter; however, reflect for a moment and perhaps you can appreciate the amount of language we miss when we cannot see, and the detrimental effect this may have on the developing language of a young child. And again, what of the language of the child who is emotionally disturbed or mentally ill, with sometimes unacceptable destructive or hyperactive behaviour; or just as worrying, the one who withdraws? Then there is stammering, which has a history almost as old as mankind. We know from records that the eminent Athenian, Demosthenes, filled his mouth with stones to overcome his stammer and went on to become the greatest orator of his time. I would certainly not suggest you follow his example, but I do know that it is a condition which most frequently begins in early childhood. Although therapists know of no cure, working with parents when their children are very young may well prevent a life-long disability.

HEARING LOSS

When a child fails to develop language in the usual way, one of the first factors we would consider is whether or not that child has a hearing loss. A large amount of research exists on the subject, and we know how even a fairly minor hearing loss, occurring recurrently early in childhood, can have devastating effects on language acquisition. There are two main types of hearing loss:

1 conductive hearing loss
2 sensori-neural hearing loss

These are described according to where damage—known as a lesion—has occurred in the ear. Both are long and complicated words, but as I shall be talking about them throughout this section, it is better that you are acquainted with them now.

With a *conductive hearing loss* there is a problem with the transmission of sound through the outer or middle ear (see Figure 13). Sounds that are of a high pitch are referred to as high frequency sounds and those of a low pitch, low frequency sounds. Frequency is measured in cycles per second (CPS), so that a high number 1,000cps is a much higher-pitch sound than, say, one at 250cps. Incoming sound, with this kind of hearing loss, loses its intensity (loudness) as all frequencies tend to be evenly affected; sounds are heard as quieter and relatively undistorted. If you want to experience the effect of conductive hearing loss, the closest you can get to it is by putting your fingers in your ears.

With a *sensori-neural hearing loss*, damage has occurred in the inner ear or to the auditory nerve, and whereas most conductive hearing losses can be improved or cured by medical or surgical treatment, the same is not true of this type of hearing loss. It is unfortunately permanent, although a

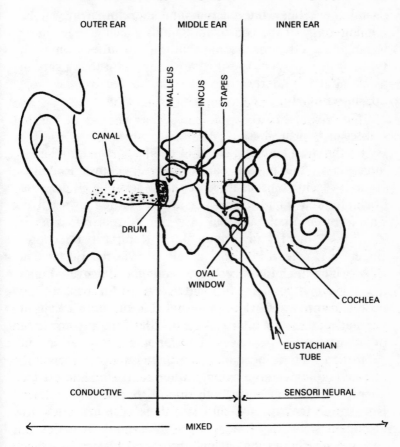

Figure 13. The human ear and types of hearing loss.
Reproduced by courtesy of A. Webster (C. McConnell, 1987).

great deal can be done nowadays to reduce its effect. Higher frequency sounds are usually more affected than those of a lower frequency. This difference or imbalance causes distortion, reminiscent of the sort you might experience when trying to have a conversation with someone in another room when the door is shut. You can hear what they are saying by recognising the patterns or 'tunes' of language, but you cannot understand, because those important high frequency sounds have been filtered out, and therefore you will be missing many of the consonant sounds which give meaning to language. Of course, some children can suffer from both types of hearing loss, and it is most important that a careful assessment is undertaken if they are to receive the most appropriate help.

Causes of Hearing Loss
By far the most common cause of conductive hearing loss is infection in the middle ear, commonly known as 'otitis media'; recent statistics indicate that a startling 80 per cent of children have had at least one attack before they are five. This is often a complication of a cold, throat infection or 'flu virus—what is known as an 'upper respiratory infection'. Infection is spread into the middle ear via the Eustachian tube, which in children is shorter and more horizontal than in adults, and connects the middle ear to the back of the nose and throat. It has the unusual task of being a kind of ventilation shaft for the middle ear. All of us, at some time or other, have experienced the 'popping' sensation in our ears when we have been in an aeroplane that is descending, and on landing emerge feeling rather deaf; after a while the air pressure equalises on both side of the ear drum, which is when you feel the 'pop' and, with relief, can hear properly again.

The Eustachian tube not only provides a means by which infection can travel, but its lining can also very easily become infected. As it then cannot do its job properly, various things may happen. The lining of the middle ear becomes swollen and infected and produces pus, which in some cases causes a build-up of pressure. This in turn causes the ear drum to rupture; but before this occurs the poor child has suffered severe earache and hearing loss in that ear. Results may not be as catastrophic as this. In other words, the ear drum does not always rupture, but even so earache, however minor, is a very unpleasant and invariably painful experience.

If the middle ear is unventilated, the ear drum will be

sucked in because of the imbalance in air pressure, and no doubt you've all experienced this with a cold. It becomes stretched and taut, and no longer vibrates as freely as before in response to sound waves. A watery-like fluid, which under normal circumstances would drain away through the Eustachian tube, may fill up the middle ear space and this will interfere with the movement of the tiny bones which respond to sound waves. Sometimes, if otitis media persists, either from lack of, or only partial success of treatment by drugs, the middle ear fluid becomes much thicker in consistency. As a result the hearing loss persists and an operation is needed to ventilate the middle ear artificially.

'Glue ear' is a condition in which there is fluid in the middle ear, without any symptoms of infection such as earache, and the cause may not be known. There has been a great deal of publicity about this condition in the media, regarding the most effective method of treatment. Many parents find the prospect of perhaps more than one operation for their child overwhelming, and as a result have turned to alternative medicine for treatment.

There are other possible causes of this type of hearing loss, the most obvious being a build-up of wax in the outer ear, or the presence of some other 'foreign body', such as a bead! Young children are insatiably curious about their ears and are prone to putting small objects in them, to see what will happen. Any of these are easily removed by your family GP.

Children with certain genetic disorders, such as Down's Syndrome, often suffer from conductive hearing loss, owing to external ear abnormalities and unusual nose, throat and Eustachian tube development. Children with 'cranio-facial' (head-face) abnormalities, such as cleft palate, are also more prone to hearing problems than other children, and it is suspected that this is associated with poor Eustachian tube function.

Sensori-Neural Hearing Loss

Fortunately, sensori-neural hearing loss is nothing like as common as conductive hearing loss; approximately two to three children in 5,000 have this more severe form of deafness as a result of permanent damage to the inner ear or auditory nerve. Of these, it is thought that at least half will have an inherited form of deafness, although this does not necessarily mean that deaf children will be born into families where deafness of this kind is commonplace. It is quite possible for one or even both parents to be carriers of the responsible gene, without being affected themselves.

During pregnancy, developing babies are very susceptible to viral infections like influenza, contracted by their mothers. You will remember that if the mother has German measles, known as the rubella virus, during the first three to four months of pregnancy, there is a high risk of the unborn child being affected. Among the handicaps which may result is a severe impairment of hearing, caused by damage to the inner ear. Not so many years ago, an epidemic of German measles would have meant a certain increase in the numbers of severely-impaired children, and it is for this reason that there is now a national vaccination programme for teenage girls. A word of caution, though, among those groups who have not been vaccinated: rubella is still a common cause of sensori-neural hearing loss.

Difficulties at the time of birth may also result in hearing loss, due to damage to the nerve cells in what is called the auditory pathway, which means any part of the nervous system associated with the function of hearing. This type of damage is caused by a lack of oxygen. Jaundice, a condition in which the child is characteristically yellow, caused by a mismatch between the blood groups of the mother and child, can also produce this type of deafness.

Premature babies are also at risk, since they are more likely to be injured during birth, be susceptible to contracting infections and suffer lack of oxygen, due to their untimely entry into the world. Sadly, children can become deaf during childhood, and perhaps one of the commonest causes is meningitis, although other childhood illnesses such as mumps, measles and chickenpox can also lead to deafness.

Assessment of Hearing Loss

Since the effects of deafness can be so devastating, tremendous efforts are being made to identify hearing loss at an early stage. There have been recent developments in which new-born babies are screened to check their hearing 'adequacy'. Amongst the professionals involved in this work, opinions differ as to whether all new-born babies should be tested, or only those from baby units considered to be at highest risk of deafness. At the present time, various interesting techniques are being developed and research trials undertaken to assess which offers the most workable method. So far, these techniques are only being used with 'at risk' new-born babies.

At risk babies continue to have their hearing carefully monitored throughout their first months, but for the rest, the majority, their hearing is not checked until they are approximately seven to eight months old, when health visitors routinely screen their responses to everyday sounds. It is known as a 'distraction' test and many parents with young children will recall having this done. Children are not screened again until they start school at the age of five years, although health visitors routinely check children at the age of three, when they take the opportunity to enquire about hearing, language, eyesight, behaviour—in fact about development in general.

The practice of regularly monitoring a population in order to identify health and developmental difficulties is now being challenged. Is it really necessary for every child to be seen, since we know that the majority are found not to have any problems? Equally, we have to ask ourselves, what happens if we only screen 'at risk' or targeted groups of children? Are we right to jeopardise all the others, whose hearing will not have been screened, but who may have a hearing loss?

Consider the destructive effect of this on their lives, language and learning, as well as on their families.

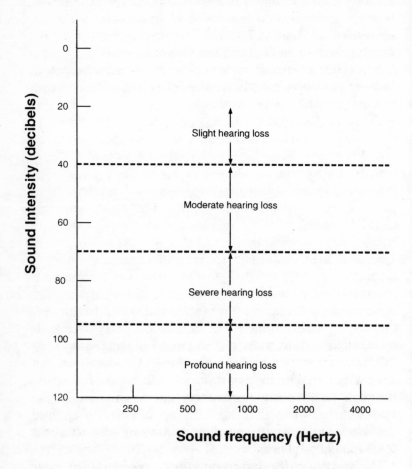

Figure 14. Degrees of hearing loss.

When children reach the age of five years, they are given a 'pure tone' test, as part of the initial school medical examination. This is different from other tests in that it only expects the child to listen for one tone at a particular frequency, rather than a word, which is made up of a whole group of tones at many different frequencies. To 'pass' this test, children must make a specific response, like posting a brick in a box, to tones at a particular degree of loudness, usually 20–25dB, across a range of frequencies which are important for hearing speech. The results are noted on a graph called an audiogram (see Figure 15).

For children who are either suspected or at risk of having hearing loss, more complicated in-depth tests will be needed, in order to find out the following:

— whether or not there is a hearing loss;

— the level of hearing right across the range of frequencies for each ear;

— where the damage has occurred;

— and, if at all possible, to discover the cause.

Effects of Hearing Loss on Speech and Language
Since the majority of conductive hearing losses are neither severe nor irreversible, many of us could be misled into believing they do not have detrimental effects on children's speech and language learning. In fact, the opposite is true, especially if a child has repeated attacks of middle ear infection at a critical time in his language development—at that early stage in the first few years of life, when he needs to discriminate between speech sounds and is learning words very rapidly.

If a child does not hear speech clearly there will be a marked delay in his development of speech sounds, as well as a general backwardness in other aspects of language development. The sounds most often affected are those which are inherently quieter or weaker—the 'hissy' sounds such as 'f', 'v', 's', 'z', nasal sounds like 'm' and 'n', and frequently word endings are missed. When a child enters school it is highly likely that a mild hearing loss will be a problem, because of the inevitable noisy conditions. We have all experienced having a cold and being a bit deaf as

Figure 15.

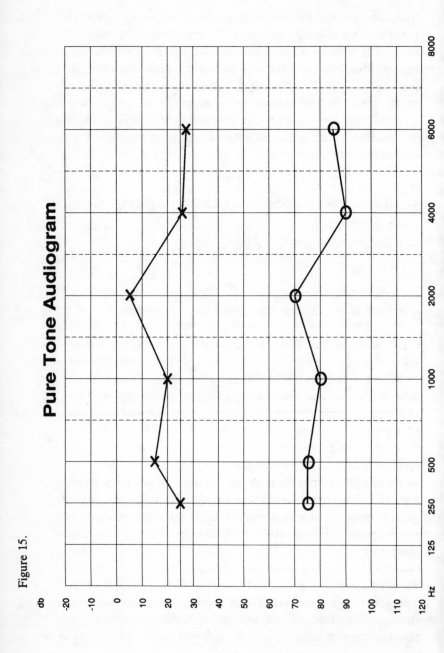

Pure Tone Audiogram

a result of this, then finding we can hear very little of a companion's conversation at the local pub, when everyone is talking, music is playing and the TV is on. It is no different for a child with a relatively minor hearing loss, when he goes to school. If undetected, a hearing loss may also cause inattention, bad behaviour or, at worst, the child is unable to cope with any kind of learning and refuses to participate.

Children with mild hearing losses may have poorer vocabularies than normal, and may be restricted in their use and understanding of words and grammar. Go into any classroom and it soon becomes obvious how important language is, even for the simplest of activities. A child could easily misunderstand questions and so do the wrong thing or give the wrong answer, and even if he does understand, he probably won't have the language to put his ideas into words. Intelligent children may seriously under-achieve, because they will be handicapped by poor language and speech—the one thing they need in order to learn effectively.

Signs to Look For That Indicate a Hearing Loss
In school, we are frequently asked by teachers what signs to look for, which might indicate that a child has a hearing loss. Although the following signs may also be present with children who have normal hearing, they should forewarn us of a possible hearing loss.

Speech is difficult to understand
A child's poor speech may be a direct result of a hearing loss and there are several reasons why it might be unintelligible—maybe because speech sounds are not clearly heard, or perhaps because the child has poor vocabulary and grammar.

Lack of attention
The child seems to be unaware of what is going on around him and has difficulty in maintaining attention over even a short period of time.

Responds differently on different days
Be aware of children who appear to be alert and responsive
on some days and not on others, and as a result may have
been branded as just naughty. On poor days their hearing
will be down and even on good days their listening may be
poor, as a result of poorly developed listening skills.

Doesn't always understand
Teachers usually become aware of a child who has difficulty
understanding, when he is asked to carry out a command
and then proceeds to do something totally unrelated. Children try to make sense of what they hear, but if the message
is difficult to hear, they will do what they think they hear.

Watches speaker's face intently
Children with hearing loss come to rely heavily on visual
clues to help them understand and, strange as it may seem,
they do actually 'hear' better when they can read lips and
facial expression.

Responds 'when he wants to'
Children who hear some frequencies better than others may
appear to be selective in what they respond to. For example,
they might look when a door opens, but not when teacher
asks a question.

Does not appear to hear speech in noisy surroundings
A child with a mild hearing loss may well be able to hear
speech from teacher or mum when it's quiet, but once the
background becomes noisy, he may fail to hear. At home
the problem could be the TV or stereo, and at school, the
usual chit-chat which goes on in an ordinary class.

Speaks very loudly or quietly
This sort of behaviour should alert us to the possibility of a
child not hearing his own voice normally, and the urgent
need to have his hearing checked.

Poor behaviour

A child who becomes irritable, unusually aggressive, easily upset, withdraws, or is just listless, should not be dismissed as simply 'difficult'. It may be he has a hearing loss and the behaviour we are noticing is his way of coping with it.

For children with sensori-neural hearing loss, as with those who have conductive hearing loss, it is not their capacity to learn language which is the problem, but rather the opportunity to experience spoken language, in order to learn it. Sadly, amplification will not resolve the problem for children with sensori-neural hearing loss; you need to remember that the child's hearing cannot be restored by this method, because damage to nerves is irreparable. Having said that, there are very few children with this type of hearing loss who in some way or another cannot derive benefit from hearing aids.

It is never too soon to start providing advice and help both to the child and the family, especially when you recall the early bonds of communication which are made between mother and child, and on which verbal language is built. It is often at this very early stage that a deaf child's language development may be disrupted. Nowadays both speech therapists and teachers of the deaf will be involved in helping the child cope with his hearing impairment.

It is very difficult to describe what a child with a hearing loss sounds like, because they are all so different. Most people are familiar with a severely hearing impaired child's speech, for it is frequently unintelligible, not only because speech sounds are poorly articulated, distorted or omitted, but also because other aspects of language are not used in the normal way. Normal rhythms and tunes of language are impaired.

Education and Deaf Children

It may surprise you to know that children with hearing impairment are usually educated with normally hearing children. I wonder how many parents realise this and, if so, do they think it is a good idea? Well it is not as unusual as you think; for the most part educationalists and therapists agree that, wherever possible, children with more severe hearing losses, as well as those with mild to moderate losses of the conductive sort, should be educated in mainstream schools. Most teachers are alert to the child who may have a less severe loss, but even so, they may not necessarily have the skills to teach them. Fortunately, specialist teachers are already employed by all LEAs; although their first responsibility is to children with more severe hearing losses and the staff working with them, they are always available to give advice on other children.

If a child needs even more specialist support, to cope with problems that are more complex, there are small classes attached to certain mainstream schools, rather like language units, which provide specialist teaching, whilst at the same time giving advice and training to mainstream staff. Under these circumstances, the children have the best of both worlds, by spending part of their time in these classes and then integrating for the rest of the day, in classes with children of their own age.

Not all children whose hearing losses are severe make the best progress in a mainstream school, even with all the help that is provided by a unit. For them, attending a special school for hearing impaired children is by far the most sensible choice. It is, however, only a minority who would benefit from this kind of education, and since the whole intention of the 1981 Education Act was to keep and support special needs children in a mainstream school, increasingly the need for children to attend these specialist schools is being questioned by the LEAs who pay for them. On the other hand, most parents seem satisfied with the education their children are receiving at these schools.

Not so long ago, speech therapists in this country were not involved in any way with children who had severe hearing impairment, although we have always worked with children who had mild to moderate hearing losses. Colleagues in other countries find this very odd, since therapists study the whole field of hearing impairment in their education and training. The situation has changed markedly over the last ten years, with our colleagues, the teachers of the deaf, increasingly acknowledging our expertise in the field of language impairment, irrespective of the causes.

The question of whether deaf children should or should not be taught manual signing remains unresolved, causing considerable anguish. There are still certain specialist schools which insist on all children learning language through the aural method, and in practice this means they must learn using their very inadequate hearing. For many children, with improved technology, this may well be the best way of learning speech and language and learning in school, but certainly not for all. Children are different and learn in different ways; as therapists we would expect them to be taught using a variety of techniques, depending on what is best for each child, including the use of manual signing.

As a profession, speech therapists are delighted that at last our expertise in the field of hearing impairment is being requested in many schools and units. As a result, many speech and language therapy departments will now have a member of staff who specialises in hearing impairment. The job would entail working in any mainstream school units for hearing impaired children, whilst at the same time giving advice to other staff. Parents may be aware that independent schools employ their own therapists.

The majority of children with hearing impairment, those with the more mild conductive losses, will be seen by the therapist at your local clinic, and if extra help or advice is needed she will ask the specialist therapist for assistance.

VISUAL IMPAIRMENT

Speech and language therapists do not see very many children who are visually impaired, at least compared to the numbers of children with other kinds of disability. Visual

loss in children can be anything from a mild degree of short-
sightedness to those who are described as 'registered blind'
and have no sight at all. Then again, it can be associated
with more complex disabilities such as cerebral palsy, and
so the therapist may already be working with children whose
visual loss is part of such a condition.

You may be wondering what the other causes are of visual
impairment. Perhaps you already know that some abnormalities of the eye are inherited, and I am quite sure many
of you will be familiar with the term 'cataract', a clouding
of the lens of the eye, mainly associated with older people;
however, it can sometimes happen that babies are born with
this condition. Some children, of course, will lose their sight
through accidents or disease, such as a tumour of the optic
nerve.

Rather like mild hearing loss, the majority of children
with visual impairment have eye conditions which are not
severe enough to cause serious problems with other aspects
of their learning. We are fortunate that the routine medical
screening carried out at the local health clinic or in school,
which most of you with children have experienced, is likely
to identify most of the visual handicaps. Children will then
be prescribed glasses, given the appropriate treatment and
medication for the problem.

Language and Visual Impairment
In the same way that children with hearing impairment miss
out on those vital early social dialogues with mum, so do
children with visual impairment. According to Dr Michel
Odent, one of the world's leading exponents of natural child-
birth, eye contact should take place immediately after
birth—even before the umbilical cord is cut—in order to
promote that early bonding between mother and child. From
an early stage in the child's life, mother and baby share not
only looking at each other, but also at objects and actions
around the child. They share the focus of interest.

But when a child cannot see, many of these early experiences of sharing are missed. It will also be difficult for a baby to do all the usual things such as reaching and grasping, becoming mobile and finding out about the world, and understanding that, if objects are hidden, it does not mean they no longer exist. The concepts a child has about the world and everything in it depend on his ability to experience it in many ways, and at the same time to tie language to those experiences.

A friend of mine related the story of how, when she went swimming, she could not hear as well as usual, and in fact became so concerned about this that she went to see her doctor. He asked her all the usual questions that might give him some clue as to why this was happening, and in the end, somewhat puzzled, sent her away to have her hearing checked. To her surprise she was found to have perfect hearing, so she raised her concerns with the audiologist who, being a perceptive person, asked my friend if she wore glasses. She thought the audiologist somewhat weird to have asked this rather odd question, but on admitting that she wore contact lenses, she was told that this was the cause of her problem.

The only time she ever needed to remove her contact lenses was when she went swimming, and of course the audiologist was quite right: just like children with visual impairment, my friend could not easily see people's faces, their expressions, their lip movements and shapes. Her lack of vision interfered with the whole process of communication. The big difference was that she had already learned language and children with visual impairment have not.

So impaired vision for a child may well mean that:

— He has fewer words than normal.
— He takes a little longer to acquire grammatical constructions.
— He may not acquire the meaning of language as quickly as able-bodied children.

Speech and language therapists will provide parents with

ideas on how to manage and improve their children's language, emphasising the urgent need to make experiences as rich and varied as possible in order to compensate for the huge amount a child would normally learn by seeing things. They will also give advice on the need to give a running commentary on what is going on, to make up for a child's lack of sight.

EMOTIONAL AND BEHAVIOURAL DISTURBANCE

Something like 50 per cent of all children with language difficulties have behaviour problems, a statistic we cannot dismiss but which causes much concern to therapists, since there is often doubt in our minds over which came first, the language delay or the behavioural difficulty. Think about it for a moment: if a child does not develop language in the normal way, he may well become disturbed about it and express himself in an antisocial way. From very early in life, babies who are unresponsive can be frustrating to their parents, and we know how important it is for mother and child to have that early communication. It has been shown in various research projects how a lack of response from a baby—no coos or smiles—eventually affects the quality and variety of parental communication with him.

As the child matures and becomes aware of what he wants and needs but is unable to express himself, he becomes increasingly frustrated. At some time or another we have all been in the situation when we desperately want to say something and cannot find the right words. For a child who has poor language this happens all the time, and once in school, a verbally demanding place, to his dismay he finds his lack of speech and language a barrier to making friends, as well as participating and being accepted by the group. As one might predict, all this can increase antisocial behaviour.

Peter and Jasper had very similar speech and language problems, but the relationship between these and their behaviour difficulties was rather different. Peter had a severe pronunciation problem and dealt with it by fluctuating between tantrums and outbursts of frustration, resulting in damage to both his toys and his poor mother. In between he would withdraw into virtual silence, unwilling to be asked, yet again, to repeat what he said and still be misunderstood. With help for his speech and careful handling of his behaviour, Peter began to make progress, and consequently his antisocial behaviour virtually ceased. At last he could be understood and he was willing to enter into conversations. So there was little doubt that it was his poor speech that was the cause of his behaviour difficulties.

On Jasper's first visit to the language unit he appeared to be a quiet, well-behaved little boy who said very little, whom we knew had severe speech and language problems. Here, we felt, was our ideal candidate. That perception was to change when he joined the class and began to show how disturbed he really was. It began with Jasper throwing anything that was available. Even chairs would be thrown, but more seriously, children were attacked without any particular provocation. Our anxiety grew when we observed Jasper's violent and sometimes explicitly overt sexual toy play. It was only later, when we learned that Jasper's name had been on what is known as the child protection register, for neglect and suspected physical abuse, that we began to have some insight into the possible causes of his severe communication problem. Speech therapists must constantly be aware of the many reasons why a child may have behaviour and emotional problems.

In the case of children whose behaviour problems have a less serious origin than those of Jasper, the cause and effect link is not always so clear. Often poor behaviour is just one of several problems and not necessarily the cause of speech and language difficulties. There are a few children who, regardless of all our efforts, resist using speech. You may have heard the term 'elective mutism', in which the child is known to be able to communicate but chooses not to do so.

It is without doubt a severe disability, and can be very resistant to help not only from therapists, but also from psychologists and psychiatrists. There have been cases documented, where the condition has persisted into adulthood. However, just occasionally, very shy children can appear to be elective mutes, especially when they go to school and find the experience totally overwhelming. Usually by the end of their first two or three terms they have begun to talk.

It is not uncommon for children who have a mental illness to experience speech and language problems; again, for therapists it is often difficult to decide if the child has a specific difficulty, or whether his frequently odd language is a result of his strange behaviour. It would be most unusual for therapists to attempt to work with children who are neglected or who have emotional or behaviour problems, without consulting psychologists or psychiatrists who have far more knowledge of how to manage these often complex difficulties.

Many children with emotional and behaviour difficulties are seen by therapists at a local clinic, but those who are under five may attend a special group at a child development centre or a small assessment class, particularly if there is doubt about the cause of their problems. Once of school age, they frequently stay in a mainstream school, with extra teaching time to help with their learning and communication difficulties, usually with an ancillary helper to assist in the classroom.

If this is unsuccessful, which might happen if a child's problems persist, most LEAs provide special units which the children attend either part- or full-time. Sometimes even this kind of help may be insufficient, and the intensive and specialised teaching of a special school may be needed. For therapists, where the children are educated makes little difference: if they feel they can help, they will form part of a team whose combined expertise is required to solve a child's complex emotional, behavioural and speech and language difficulties.

STAMMERING IN CHILDREN

Many of you will have listened to the popular radio programme *Just a Minute*, in which the participants talk for one minute on a particular subject, without hesitation, repetition or deviation. I don't know if you have ever tried to do it, but it is extremely difficult. You will pause, use at least half a dozen 'ers' or 'ums' and I guarantee will repeat the sound of a word, a whole word, or even a complete phrase. Listen to any politician on the *Today* programme and count how many times he says, 'The fact of the matter is . . .'

None of us, including the politicians, would be considered non-fluent, so when does this 'normal non-fluency' become a stammer? How is it recognised and what causes it? Even after 60 years of research, experts still do not know what causes a child or adult to stammer. Stammering, rather like reading difficulties, appears to run in families; however, it is not inevitable that your child will have a stammer if you or someone in your family has one.

What should parents be aware of to recognise the beginnings of a stammer? What are the characteristic symptoms? Well, sounds, syllables and words will be repeated, consonants and vowels will be prolonged, and most likely the child will pause at inappropriate times. Parents may gradually become aware of their child's stammer, and the way they describe it to therapists is fairly typical. James's mum, for example, had noticed a period when he stammered—we would call this non-fluency—which did not last but was punctuated by fluent periods, before he began to stammer all the time. Sometimes, in total contrast to this, the onset of the stammer is quite sudden, brought on, parents feel, by a traumatic experience such as an accident or illness.

One particular symptom, called 'blocking', which I have so far not mentioned, needs some explanation. Once you have heard it, you would undoubtedly consider it more distinctive than either repetition or prolongation; it is not pleasant for either the speaker or the listener. For the person who stammers, there is an increase in body tension when he attempts to say anything, but when blocking occurs there is a much greater increase in tension at a point when speech is about to be articulated. This can happen with our lips, for lip sounds 'm, b, p', or with the tongue, for 't, d, k' and 'g', when our tongue makes contact with our palate and in our larynx, better known to most of us as our Adam's apple. Our vocal folds come together to produce sound for speech, and when a block occurs no sound may come out or the block may be voiced. If any sound is made, it usually resembles a strangled groan.

Many young children go through non-fluent phases of speaking as part of normal language development, particularly around the age of three to three-and-a-half years, when they are suddenly beginning to use a lot of language. Whether or not this is considered to be a stammer depends very much on the parents' attitude. If you or someone in your family already has a stammer, or even had one as a child, you are likely to become extremely anxious and immediately assume your child has a stammer. If you react as if he has a stammer and persist with this attitude, sooner or later your child will also assume that he has a stammer.

So what do we do when a parent comes to the clinic with a child who is stammering? Parents are usually rather puzzled, some even dismayed, when we tell them that we shall be doing very little with their child, especially if he is young, but a great deal with them and the rest of the family. Our intention is to help parents to change the way in which they handle their child and his stammer; there is so much they can do to reduce the pressure on his speech—in fact on everything which is associated with communication in general—and this includes relaxing and not communicating their anxiety to their child. Nothing could be worse than telling a child to stop, take a deep breath and start again, yet this is probably one of the most usual ways in which parents react, believing they are doing the right thing.

If the situation is dealt with correctly, you will most likely see a decrease and often disappearance of the stammer. As parents, you must be prepared to do all the work, sometimes even to change your thinking and, perhaps hardest of all, persuade grandma, grandpa, aunts, uncles, cousins and friends to do likewise. One mother told a therapist colleague of her utter disbelief when she had been asked to change the way in which she dealt with her child's stammer.

'My first reaction,' she said, 'was to say, "You must be joking, it's his problem, not mine." However, I'm a polite person, so I said nothing, and anyway, I felt at the time there was nowhere else to go and this person was supposed to know all about stammering; so I thought I'd have a try, although I was not convinced it would work.'

This particular mother's reaction was not unusual, but to her and the rest of the family's credit, they did everything that was asked for her child, and the changes they made were successful.

Ideally, this kind of preventative therapy should work for every child; sadly, we know that it doesn't, but with further support from a speech and language therapist, the child with a persistent stammer can receive immeasurable help from his family. From time to time in the media we see claims made about a cure for stammering: regard these with suspicion. Therapists will give no guarantees since, so far, we know of nothing which works for everyone. We prefer to be more cautious and explain what we can do. We can give you guidance, advice and therapy. Work with us and your child will more than likely become more fluent, and if his stammer completely disappears, so much the better.

BILINGUAL CHILDREN

Under normal circumstances, for the majority of children who learn to speak several languages, there is no conflict; research shows that the only effect may be a slight delay in acquiring all the languages. So you may be wondering why the expertise of speech therapists is needed. With certain children, the fact that they speak several languages masks the difficulties they are having in learning their own language. Speaking more than one language merely complicates the situation.

Our dilemma, then, is to discover if the child has a genuine language difficulty, or if it can be accounted for by anything else. Increasingly, we are educating and training therapists who speak several languages and whose expertise can be used in the diagnosis and treatment of these children; this is particularly important in parts of the country where there are large immigrant populations.

Where a therapist is not available, we seek the help of the local 'English as a Second Language' service, which is available in most areas from the education department. They will often supply a translator who is a trained teacher, and may well already have referred the child for an assessment because of their own concerns.

Once we have decided what the problem might be, the children will receive therapy in whichever is the predominant language, usually English. Irrespective of the difficulties several languages cause, therapists cannot ignore their cultural and social implications. As often as not, it is unreasonable to suggest to certain families that it would be better for the child if they could speak only in English, because the mother and grandparents communicate in another language and cannot actually speak English.

In most instances, we are fortunate enough to have the help and advice of other professionals who have a great deal of experience of working with immigrant families; at the same time, therapists are gradually finding ways in which they too can work more effectively, using the knowledge and expertise that already exists within the profession. It is an area of work which, until recent years, has been underestimated and is only now receiving its full recognition.

9 Integration

Ask half-a-dozen different people what they understand by integration and you will get as many different answers. Its advocates are passionate in its defence, but equally its adversaries are dismissive of its claims and view attempts at integration as 'disintegration'. Certainly, you only need ask the question in a school staff room to be convinced of how differently it is interpreted, not only by teachers but by LEAs from Land's End to the Shetlands. After listening to many arguments between teachers over the years, one realises what a complex subject it is.

Look up the meaning of the word 'integration' in the dictionary, and it tells you it is 'the act of combining or amalgamating'. Yet in its widest sense integration implies far more: it encompasses the whole idea of equality—that all men and women are equal, regardless of sex, race, creed, colour or religion. You could of course argue that this was never the intention of integration, but you do not have to go farther back than Martin Luther King and the struggle of the black people of the southern United States to have their children integrated into white schools, to appreciate that this is no longer the case. The argument goes something like this: equality, be it educational, social, emotional or of opportunity, can only be achieved within mainstream society, by being made available to all people.

So you can perhaps begin to understand how, in purely educational terms, integration is interpreted by its most zealous advocates as all children being placed in a mainstream class, irrespective of their disability, whilst at the other end of the integration spectrum it is argued that those with disabilities can only be prepared for life by being educated in a special environment. It is essential to realise that there is a wide diversity of opinion on the integration issue.

To have a real understanding of how we perceive integration, it is helpful to see how educational provision for children with disabilities—today's correct term is 'special needs'—has evolved.

THE HISTORICAL BACKGROUND

Many of you may be surprised to learn that, in this country, special education for the 'handicapped', or more accurately, pupils with 'special educational needs', is quite recent. Two hundred years ago, in 1790, Henry Braidwood set up the first school for the deaf and was followed the next year by Henry Dunnett with a school for the blind. Throughout the 1800s more special schools opened for children who were blind and deaf, and these were followed, as universal elementary education spread, with schools for children with learning difficulties.

By the beginning of this century, it was increasingly apparent that the school boards needed to be replaced by another form of administration which would take responsibility for a far greater number of schools; so the Local Education Authorities came into being. These, however, continued developing the separate system of education which had already been established. In the light of what we now know about children with disabilities, we may well wonder why this was done. Although it is not easy to envisage, we need to ask ourselves about the Victorians' understanding of handicap if we are to find some clues. At that time people believed that a child's handicap was an unalterable characteristic of that child, so it made sense to develop separate educational systems—one for the able and the other for the 'handicapped'.

The 1944 Education Act

In recent history there have surely been few pieces of legislation to compare with the 1944 Education Act which, as a result of its diverse recommendations, was to change the lives of millions of people and give them new and undreamed of opportunities. For the first time, integration was at least given some serious consideration, since it was suggested that the less severely handicapped, who in fact now, as then, make up the majority of children with disabilities, should be educated in ordinary schools. Regrettably, as is often the way with good intentions, they were never fulfilled since, following the Second World War, Britain's funds were meagre. Amid the problems of finding school accommodation, together with the shortage of trained teachers, integration was hardly considered.

Local Education Authorities which were able to purchase old town and country houses relatively cheaply found it an easier option to educate handicapped pupils separately. So the two systems, ordinary schools and special schools, continued to run in parallel, with different expectations for children and different ways of educating them.

Our ideas on how children with disabilities should be assessed has changed radically in recent years, but between 1944 and the 1960s the guidance given in the Education Act was followed. At that time, what is now understood as the 'medical model' was used—that is, the belief that a 'handicap' had a direct medical cause—which today we realise is far too simplistic an idea to explain children's disabilities. The responsibility of assessing a child was undertaken by a medical officer who then both organised and allocated special education, according to categories of 'handicap' which were outlined in the 1944 Act. At that time, there were eleven categories, but these were later modified to ten. Certain children, considered to be ineducable, were passed on to the Health Authority and categorised as 'severely subnormal'. That children's futures could be determined in this primitive way by society in recent times is unbelievable.

By the beginning of the 1960s, with the abolition of the 11+ examination and the establishment of comprehensive schools, a new and enlightened wave of thinking provided the opportunity to discuss the many concerns associated with the whole concept of a separate system of 'special' education. At the time, international growing concern for human rights focused attention on the broader concept of integration. Also, other countries, particularly the United States and Scandinavia, were adopting extremely enlightened policies towards what they called the 'normalisation' of the handicapped—in other words, looking at how they could be included, rather than excluded, by the rest of society.

Even today, however, people with disabilities will tell you how impossibly difficult it is for them at times to be accepted as real human beings; to be accepted by the rest of society in shops, theatres, the workplace, in fact in all aspects of life. Even when there is legislation to support their claims, it is frequently ignored. Thirty years ago the whole idea was entirely new.

Armed with the evidence of reforms taking place in other countries, active pressure groups in this country increased the pace of change. Eventually, in 1970, another Act of Parliament removed the iniquitous division between those who were considered educable in school and those who were not.

The Warnock Report
Many professionals and parents expressed grave doubts about the way in which children with handicaps were classified, and the validity of the ten categories outlined in the Education Act, that were used for this procedure. The government of the day reacted to these concerns in 1978, by setting up the Warnock Committee to take a completely new look at the needs of children with handicaps and how they might best be approached.

Over the years it had become apparent that using medical

terms for describing 'handicap' was not especially helpful in deciding the best education for a child. It had been found, for instance, that the degree of a child's handicap did not necessarily relate to his intellectual ability; for example, children with quite severe physical handicap could just as well be educated in a mainstream school—providing, of course, they were given the correct amount of extra help.

So Warnock moved away from the 'medical model', and instead decided to use a child's development and educational principles as a means of assessment; in other words, in the future it would be the child's ability, rather than his disability, which would be given the greatest consideration.

A wholly new concept of 'special education needs' was suggested, which would take into consideration everything in the child's life that would have any relevance to his progress. It was also recommended that, as far as possible, a child should be given the opportunity to learn the same range of subjects as any able-bodied child. This was, without doubt, a totally new idea which, incidentally, has been taken one step further with the introduction of the National Curriculum. Once again, attention had been drawn to the integration of children with 'handicaps', or, as the new term suggested, 'with special education needs'.

1981—The Next Step

In a way, this particular milestone in education did not achieve what it set out to do, for instead of clarifying exactly what constituted 'special education needs', there was to follow a great deal of debate, arising from the imprecise language used in this particular piece of legislation. It stated that a child has 'special education needs' if he has a learning difficulty that 'is significantly greater than the majority of children of the same age'.

This rather vague description did not help anyone. Who was to decide what constituted 'the majority of children'— was this 60 per cent or 70 per cent or even 90 per cent?

Even more contentious, what was meant by a 'significantly greater' learning difficulty?

It was followed by an equally vague statement that LEAs were expected to place these children in ordinary schools and provide help for them, but only 'if this is compatible with the child's education needs, the efficient education of the other children with whom he or she is being educated and the efficient use of resources.' This means that children can attend local schools, so long as the schools can meet their needs and their presence does not interfere with the education of the other children.

This is a wonderful list of opt-out clauses for schools, who very reasonably could argue that the child is too difficult, or that they haven't enough money, or that it would be detrimental to the education of the other children.

For the first time in any piece of educational legislation, parents were to be regarded as partners; they were to be involved in the future of their children's education by being actively consulted at every stage of a 'statement' of educational need. Irrespective of the shortcomings of the Act, it was excellent. Here at last was something parents had been campaigning about for many years. They were now to be included when decisions were being made concerning their children's educational future.

Sadly, regardless of the intentions of the Act and its far-reaching implications, this was not the case for many parents, for, as they were to find out, there were many problems still to be overcome. A parent described the struggle to get help for her son in the mainstream school as an 'assault course', which sounds rather extreme; but as she explained, no sooner had one problem been solved than another emerged. This mother feels that she was misled and misunderstood, ignored and harassed, for the simple reason that she did not agree with the professionals. They wanted her son to attend a special school, while she preferred a mainstream school. It took three years for the situation to be resolved, when the family won an appeal against the LEA.

Although the 1981 Act stated that more children from special schools should be educated in mainstream, for some unaccountable reason there has only been a small drop in the numbers of children in segregated educational placements. As I see it, one of the reasons for this is that everyone has a different idea of both the meaning and the full implications of integration. The main standpoints could be summarised as follows:

Suggestion One
According to this view, integration is seen in terms of the kind of relationship or association special needs children have with the ordinary school. It is described by three terms—'locational', 'social' and 'functional'.

— 'Locational' means where the children are physically located in the school, which might be in segregated special units or in ordinary classes with the mainstream pupils.

— 'Social' means that children have play, mealtimes, assembly and other out-of-class activities with the mainstream children—in other words, they have opportunities of joining in activities which are not actually in the classroom.

— 'Functional' is the fullest form of integration, in which both of the other forms of integration—locational and social—eventually lead to special needs children joining mainstream classes for all or part of the day.

Suggestion Two
This sees integration as a 'continuum', a word I have used previously because it is so descriptive; you must imagine a line which represents integration, with one end indicating least and the other most amount of integration. At the one end, that shown as 'most', the child is in an ordinary class with extra teaching or ancillary help, and at the other, that

shown as 'least', at a special school which has links with ordinary school.

Most		Integration		Least
1	2	3	4	5

The numbers represent various forms of integration as follows:

1—The child is in an ordinary class with extra help in the classroom.
2—The child is in an ordinary class, but is withdrawn for extra teaching.
3—The child combines attending a special class in the mainstream school part-time, with an ordinary class part-time.
4—The child is in a special class in ordinary school full-time.
5—The child is in a special class located away from a mainstream school, but having contact with ordinary school.

Not everyone agrees that this is a 'continuum', since a child at number 3 may be more 'integrated' than, say, the child at 1. They would argue that placing a child in an ordinary class, with help, does not guarantee he will be accepted or be part of the class. Also as I mentioned on p. 207, the degree to which a child is integrated does not necessarily reflect the degree of severity of his disability. We know there are severely disabled children at point 1 and less disabled at point 5.

Suggestion Three
This is more radical than either *One* or *Two* and advocates all children leaving special schools and becoming full members of ordinary schools. It is argued that schools must completely reorganise for these pupils, in order to take account of their special needs. Instead of being a school for only the majority of the children in the community, it should be for all children, irrespective of their special needs. This

view is favoured by those who see it as society's responsibility to change and adapt, rather than that those with disabilities should adapt to society. The problem should not be solved by the disabled but by society. If this was the official line, you will appreciate that even the most sympathetic of schools would need to change their thinking radically.

So this is what the experts say. You may agree or you may not—no matter, it is for the individual to make his own choice. Integration, as far as I am concerned, is an evolutionary process through which a child passes, with the long-term objective of becoming a fully integrated member of society. In all of this, though, it is the child's needs which are of paramount impoitance. As the child's needs change, so the provisions for the child must change accordingly. You might say that children don't necessarily need integration—remember, integration is a means, not an end in itself. What they need is education. It is regrettable that integration has acquired the reputation of being either 'good' or 'bad', depending on whom you talk to and their point of view. Consequently, we have to remind ourselves who integration is for. In the educational environment it is about children; after all, a wrong decision about where and how a child should be educated is a failure all round—for the child, the family, the school, and of course, not least, for the whole process of integration itself.

The intention of the 1981 Education Act was to give children with special educational needs the opportunity to be educated in mainstream school, and to outline clearly the nature of those needs. This was accomplished through the 'Statement of Need'.

THE 'STATEMENT'

Many parents whose children have severe communication impairment, as well as those whose children's communication problem is associated with some other disability, may be familiar with a procedure which was introduced under the 1981 Education Act. It is correctly titled a 'Statement of Need', but is known to everyone as a 'statement'. It describes the child's needs and the proposals for meeting those needs. 'Advice,' as it is called, which in fact is a report, is collected from everyone who is involved with a child, including the parents who, as well as making their own contribution, at the same time have a legal right not only to do this, but to be involved at every stage of the procedure. The statement is a five-part document which contains the following:

a) Section I gives the usual details of your child—his name, date of birth, and so on.
b) Section II gives the Local Education Authority's view of the child's special educational needs.
c) Section III details the special educational provision appropriate to meet the needs.
d) Section IV outlines the type of school considered appropriate.
e) Section V includes the speech and language therapist's report or advice. This section contains all the 'non-educational advice'.

Any suggestions, or what we would call proposals, which appear under Section V are funded by the service which has made them and not by the educational service. Once the statement is complete, it is then the responsibility of the Local Education Authority to provide for the child the kind of help outlined in the statement. It is important for parents to know that they have the right to challenge the contents of the statement.

When do Children Have Statements?
Any child, from the age of two onwards, can have a statement. Those with very obvious and severe physical or learning disabilities will receive a statement very early in life, since Education Authorities may fund children between the ages of two to five years to attend nursery schools or units,

which will cater for their special educational needs. The majority of children with special needs do not have a statement before going to school, and in fact most will not require one, because of the amount of extra help that is already available in school.

Speech and Language Therapists and Statements

Whenever a statement is being compiled, should a speech and language therapist's advice be required, there is a formal procedure to be followed. First of all the Local Education Authority will contact the Health Authority or Trust through a medical officer, whose responsibility it is to inform all other health professionals working with that particular child. This ensures that the therapist has plenty of time to write a report on the child.

Speech and language therapists have fairly strict guidelines on what they must do when they receive a request to give advice for a statement. These dictate what information should be included in a report, the distribution and, in most departments, how long the procedure should take. Therapists are asked to say what we think a child needs for his communication difficulty. Naturally, any commitment we make is undertaken in consultation with the head of department. Before sending off a report, we always confirm with parents that, in their opinion, what is written in the report is an accurate reflection of their child's difficulties.

Once all the advice has been collected by the Local Education Authority, a draft or first copy of the statement is issued to the parents for their agreement. They have fifteen days in which to consider the contents, and if they are satisfied a final statement is issued; if not, they can appeal. In most cases any early objections are considered sympathetically by the LEA.

When statementing was first introduced, the LEAs were slow to progress statements, often because they were still interpreting the legislation. Inevitably, this situation caused a great deal of distress to some parents, but happily you should now find the whole procedure taking months rather than years. If you remember how your child was working a year ago, it is likely that by now he has made considerable progress; with this in mind, every child has his statement reviewed on an annual basis. On the other hand, you may not be satisfied, and may wish to take the opportunity to ask for further help for your child. Bear in mind, too, that if a child still has a statement at the age of 13+, there is a process of mandatory reassessment.

In 1988 a minor revision of the 1981 Education Act was made, which was of specific interest to speech and language therapists but I suspect is of equal interest to parents. The amendment involved 'non-educational provision', which you will recall comes under Section V of the statement and includes every service apart from education, such as health or social services. It enabled the Local Education Authorities to provide these additional services, should they wish, without removing the responsibility for these to be provided by the Health Authority or Trust. If you think about it, this was a very positive piece of legislation, especially for speech therapists, since, in many areas where there were shortages in the service, the result has been joint-funded posts, and occasionally LEAs have funded full-time therapy posts.

An even more significant piece of legal history was made in Lancashire, as the result of a statement appeal, *Regina vs Lancashire County Council* (1989). The parents argued that it was the LEA's responsibility to provide therapy, since their child's communication disorder was interfering with his learning, and that it was therefore an 'educational', not a 'health' problem. The judges agreed with the parents; as in any legal precedent, it is a positive advance for any parents who believe their child may be in a similar situation.

Most parents are unaware not only of this judgement, but also of their right to challenge the LEA to have therapy included in their child's statement as an educational need, if they are convinced his communication disorder is interfering with learning. This means that it should appear in Section III of the statement. There is a fine subtlety of interpretation, of which parents should be aware and which may not be clear. Whether or not your child is receiving therapy from the Health Authority or Trust does not alter your right to challenge the LEA.

Children Who do Not Have Statements

Statements are expensive documents to prepare. Assembling the information on the child costs between £2,000 and £3,000; understandably, LEAs argue that not every child who has a learning difficulty requires one. So the majority of children with special educational needs do not in fact have a statement, but this does not mean they have been neglected. Once children are in school, it does not take teachers very long to notice those who are experiencing problems and to begin, fairly promptly, to give them some extra help. Every school has a 'special needs co-ordinator', with responsibility for all the children with difficulties, whether or not they have a statement. This may be fulfilled by giving the class teacher advice or by providing extra teaching time.

Some parents seem to feel that as soon as their child gets a little behind in his learning, it is time to send for the educational psychologist, rather as you would send for the doctor if you were ill. It doesn't work quite as simply as that. Let me explain what happens.

Before calling the educational psychologist, most LEAs have instructed their schools to go through a series of assessments with the child, which are graded according to degrees of difficulty. For the first assessment there will no doubt be one or two problems. Inevitably, by the time the child has failed the final assessment, the school will require an opinion from the educational psychologist.

School funding has changed in the last few years, with the devolvement of funds from the LEA to the local schools (called LMS—local management scheme); consequently, schools now have their own personalised budgets. Included in these are funds for children with special needs.

INTEGRATION AND SPECIAL PLACEMENTS

For the majority of children who have special educational needs, with or without a statement, mainstream school is where they will receive their education. It is over the two per cent who are mostly placed in special schools that there is so much disagreement. In my experience, 'place' does not give a true measure of how well a child is 'integrated'. For example, David, in his mainstream school, with great difficulties in understanding language, was shunned by the other children; failure and isolation were his everyday experience. In contrast, Mike attended a special school which had links with a local mainstream school where he spent part of his week, was accepted and felt very much at home with his friends there.

Location can be a barrier, but more often it is attitudes that really count. Children know when and by whom they are valued and accepted—not for what they do, but for who they are. It is the ideals of a school that matter, as well as its policy towards pupils who are different as a result of their disabilities, and who possibly will not be its high achievers.

It is interesting to review the various ways in which children with the most severe disabilities are given opportunities to integrate with children who do not have such problems. In some ways, children with physical disabilities can offer the greatest challenges where integration is concerned, due no doubt to the help they need from so many professionals. Ordinary schools may also have to make special provision for their physically disabled children, by way of ramps and suitable toilets.

During the fourteen or so years a physically disabled child is at school, one or more of the following placements could be offered:

- An ordinary class in mainstream school with support.
- An ordinary class in mainstream school with support, and also a 'resource base', which is a class within the school, to which children with special needs can withdraw.

- Part-time in a special class which is in a mainstream school, part-time in an ordinary class in the same school.
- Full-time in a special class in a mainstream school.
- Part-time in a day special school, part-time in a day mainstream school.
- Full-time in a day special school with 'links' to a mainstream school.
- Residential special school which has links with mainstream local schools.
- Hospital school with links to local mainstream schools.

Sometimes an LEA might have difficulty in providing this wide range of resources and have to look for it elsewhere, such as the charity-run schools. Perhaps the most important thing to remember is that the type of schooling a child receives may well change, as his needs change.

Scott is a wonderful example of this kind of progression, a child who changed dramatically over the years and so, fortunately, did his schooling. Scott contracted meningitis when he was four years old, which left him paralysed down his right side, with speech and language problems as well as a hearing impairment. At first he needed a great deal of help from many different sources—speech therapy, physiotherapy, occupational therapy, social services, the peripatetic (visiting) teacher of the deaf, as well as specialist teachers, were all involved. His parents and the Local Education Authority agreed this help could best be provided in the local day special school.

Scott thrived, made excellent progress, and within two years was attending a special class in a mainstream school, where he had speech therapy and physiotherapy. Within a further two years he was attending a mainstream class full time, with extra teaching help. The LEA actively encouraged integration as a general philosophy throughout all their schools, and as a result children felt accepted and their problems understood. Scott still has some speech problems and cannot fully use his right hand and arm, but regardless of this, he successfully passed his GCSE examinations.

In principle, the alternatives for integration available for children with other disabilities are much the same as those for children with physical disability. There are, of course, variations depending on the type of disability. It would not be viable for an LEA to have a special school for children with specific language disorder, as there would be too few children in the area to fill it. On the other hand, far greater numbers of children have learning disabilities and, at some time in their lives, a number of them will no doubt need a special school. Therefore, it makes economic sense for the LEA to have this type of provision.

Integration and Children with Speech and Language Difficulties

You will recall that about ten per cent of the nation's children experience a communication problem at some time in their lives; they will either be among the 15 per cent of children with special educational needs already in a mainstream school, or among the two per cent who are currently attending special schools.

In most areas therapists will be working with children who are attending a wide range of schools and units. As you can imagine, working with children in so many different places requires a great deal of organisation, as well as careful use of resources. Teachers are the people to whom we turn for help with some of the children with more severe problems; school is the natural place to learn and we want to capitalise on this.

One way of working with the school is to use the local clinic as the base where a child is seen at intervals of say, a month; in the meantime the school is asked to follow up a therapy programme. Robin is a good example of a child who made progress in this way. He was shy in the clinic, but enjoyed school and always wanted to please his teacher. The therapist contacted the school to enlist their co-operation, asking them to work with Robin for ten minutes a day. If there were any misunderstandings the school could call the therapist for an explanation. This way of working is shown in the chart below:

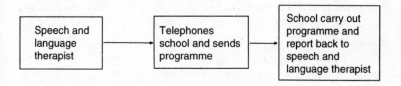

Scheme I: Working in a mainstream school

Susie was a most obliging child in therapy, but at the age of five she was still not easily putting words together in sentences. She sounded like the old-time telegrams—all the key words were there; missing were the vital small ones. With Susie, it was important for the therapist to have closer contact with the school, so that her difficulties could be explained and the way in which they might affect her learning.

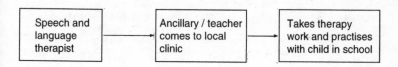

Scheme II: Working in a mainstream school

The school agreed to send one of their ancillary helpers to accompany Susie when she went to therapy, in order to watch the therapist at work and to learn more about Susie's difficulties. Occasionally, the school allowed her teacher to accompany Susie to the clinic.

Sometimes therapists make regular visits to schools, in order to discuss the problems of children like Susie, rather than rely solely on the visits of the ancillary helper. This way of working is summarised below:

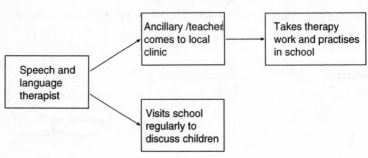

Scheme III: Working in a mainstream school

Marie had a far more severe language difficulty than either David or Susie; she also had a statement, in which the therapy department had undertaken to see her in school, as shown in the chart below:

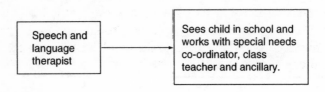

Scheme IV: Working in a mainstream school

Had Marie been living in a different part of the county, she might have had a specialist speech and language therapist and specialist teacher visiting her, rather like Scheme V below, a collaboration between the local speech and language therapy department and the Local Education Authority.

Special units and special schools always have speech and language therapists working in them, sometimes full-time, but more usually on a part-time basis. In these cases, much

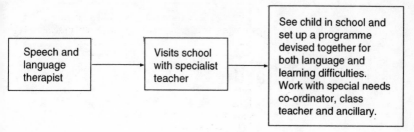

Scheme V: Working in a mainstream school

depends on the amount of funding available, and also on the numbers of children involved.

Integration will continue to engender much argument until a consensus can be reached on what it means in the area of education. Sometimes, amid the heated discussions, we tend to forget who integration is for. It is not for the adults who endlessly argue over its rights and wrongs; it is for children who have special needs. However strongly-held our beliefs, we must always try to provide the children with what is right for them and not what is right for us.

10 The Charities

The British have a reputation for forming a society when a need is recognised, and then that organisation assuming charitable status. Go into any large library and you will find a listing of charitable organisations. There are, quite literally, thousands, representing the needs of every aspect of human life.

Choosing which of these to include here was easier than I had anticipated. Surprisingly, there are very few charities which have been established purely for individuals who cannot communicate, and yet one would have thought that, in a world where communication is so important, there would have been dozens. It is perhaps a reflection of the lack of public awareness on the whole subject of communication disorder. When it is associated with other more obvious disabilities, as in, say, cerebral palsy, there is a degree of sympathy, but usually for the physical impairment and not the fact that the person cannot communicate in the usual way. In this chapter I shall outline the work of a selected number of charities which represent people who cannot communicate, as a result of a whole range of conditions.

AFASIC—Association for all Speech Impaired Children
AFASIC was founded twenty-five years ago, by a group of concerned, frustrated parents and professionals, under the direction of Mrs Margaret Greene, a highly talented, articulate and formidable speech therapist. Her experience of working with large numbers of pre-school children, particularly in London, had convinced her of the inadequate

facilities available for the diagnosis, clinical treatment, parent guidance and subsequent educational placement of children with learning difficulties stemming from the language disorder. She had gathered around her a number of colleagues who shared her concerns, and together they established a working party to prepare the way for the Association.

At that time, children with specific language disorder, who had failed to learn language in the normal way, were frequently diagnosed as 'mentally retarded', yet with appropriate help would progress at an amazing rate. It was obvious that something needed to be done to draw attention to their needs. AFASIC is a very apt title since, in the early days, the term 'aphasic' was used to describe what we now call specific language disorder.

AFASIC has grown in influence over the years, but its broad aims remain the same—to increase awareness and recognition of communication impairments, in order that there will be better medical, educational and employment/training prospects; and following this, to help children and young people to develop increased confidence and self-esteem, so enabling them in the long term to participate more fully in society. Currently there are five paid employees—Director, Administrative Secretary, Fundraiser, Education Officer and Regional Development Officer—who are all assisted by a team of volunteer workers.

Parents and children wanting further help can get advice and information on speech and language impairments. There are something like fifty local groups which provide support for families. In recent years, AFASIC has established training courses for professionals and parents, as well as very practical guidance for young people. It organises many activities, in order to give youngsters the opportunity to develop communication skills and build self-confidence. It is also active in pressing government for better diagnostic, treatment, and educational facilities.

ICAN—Invalid Children's Aid Nationwide

ICAN, previously known as the ICAA (Invalid Children's Aid Association), was founded in 1888 by Allan Graham, who was horrified at the plight of sick and disabled children in the East End of London. His concern grew from the evidence collected by workers from the Charity Organisation Society (now renamed the Family Welfare Association), of the dreadful state of many of the seriously disabled children in the metropolis. Allan Graham undertook to launch a society which would be devoted solely to the interest of disabled children, and collected around him a team of able people—doctors, clergymen, nurses, representatives of other societies and a number of dedicated ladies who were the wives or daughters of the doctors.

Over the hundred years since it was founded, ICAN has been the catalyst for the foundation of other charities devoted to specific groups of children with special needs, most notably the Spastics Society and British Dyslexia Association. Its policy has always been to work with other organisations, whether they are charitable or governmental.

Of particular interest to parents of children with specific language disorder is the work of ICAN with this group of children over the last 25 years. It has established three special schools specifically for their education and therapy, as well as giving more attention in recent years to the pre-schoolers, for whom there is now an increasing number of units.

John Horniman School, in Worthing, West Sussex, accepts children from five to nine years, whose primary disability is that of severe speech and language disorder with associated learning difficulties; it also accepts hearing impaired children with language disorder. Dawn House School, in Rainworth, Nottinghamshire, accepts children from 5–16 years with severe specific speech and language disorders, but not those with hearing loss. Along with John Horniman, the children must have at least average or above non-verbal ability, without significant emotional or behavioural problems, no physical disability or chronic medical condition. Meath House, located in Ottershaw, Surrey, accepts children aged 5–12 years, but with a wider ability range and including those with moderate additional handicaps.

ICAN is also involved in the education and further training of children and young people with other disabilities, as well as professionals who work with them. It offers support and advice to the families of children who attend its schools and nurseries.

The Spastics Society
The Spastics Society was founded in 1952 specifically for individuals who have cerebral palsy. From small beginnings it has grown into one of the largest charities working with people with cerebral palsy, their parents and carers. It has six regional offices as well as its headquarters in London, plus a network of over 700 affiliated groups. Amongst its many services, there is an advisory assessment centre for children and adults, an assessment centre for conductive education, and the innovative Cerebral Palsy Helpline, which will give you information, advice and counselling on just about anything associated with cerebral palsy.

Of particular interest to parents of children who have communication impairment, as a result of their physical disability, is the advice, support and therapy given by the speech and language therapists employed by the Society. They work with other professionals in the assessment centre, and in the seven schools run by the Society. The schools have been most innovative in their work with both children and parents, in establishing a network of 'schools for parents', where parents have the opportunity to learn alongside their children. Trengweath School in Plymouth, for example, has branched out from its school for parents, to helping many more families through its community programme. A team of professionals visits families at home, as well as giving training and advice to staff and children in mainstream school. On top of this it provides a 24-hour, seven-days-a-week respite care service, offering nursing and care support that make it possible for parents to take a break from their child.

CLAPA—Cleft Lip and Palate Association
CLAPA was founded 13 years ago by a group of 300 parents and professionals. The current chairman suggests that the statement 'if only CLAPA had been there when my child was born' aptly summarises the mood of the day on which the inaugural meeting was held. The association, like so many others, arose out of the need for information, advice and support which parents urgently require when confronted by their baby's condition. It is at this time, during those first few weeks and months, that parents, who are in an understandably shocked frame of mind, want their questions answered.

As well as parents, CLAPA has among its ranks nurses, plastic surgeons, dental specialists, psychologists, speech and language therapists and social workers, all of whom have particular experience or expertise and understanding of the needs and treatment of those with cleft lip or cleft palate, from birth, through childhood and adulthood.

CLAPA's aims are to give support especially to the parents of the new-born child, to encourage and support research into the condition and to provide ongoing education and training for professional workers, parents and the general public. The Association also aims to publish educational material, raise funds, and provide an informal link between parents and professionals. It publishes a quarterly newsletter, and also some excellent leaflets which explain a potentially complex condition in clear, simple terms. There are over 40 local CLAPA groups throughout Great Britain, but unlike other charities, the administrative staff at head office remain unpaid. CLAPA has stated its aim to improve this situation, and is currently looking at how it can establish a permanent central office, with paid staff and central fund-raising potential.

The National Autistic Society
On the initiative of a group of desperate and concerned parents, the National Society for Autistic Children was formed in 1962, modelling itself on the Spastics Society which, at that time, had been in existence for ten years. Diagnosis of the condition can still be problematical, but 30 years ago it was infinitely more difficult because of the prevailing ignorance about autism, even among the medical profession. The term 'autistic' was not well understood and children were also known as 'psychotic', or suffering from 'childhood schizophrenia'.

Knowledge and understanding of autism has moved on since then, due in no small measure to the work of the Society. It changed its name in 1982 to reflect its role in looking after the special needs of all individuals who are autistic, irrespective of age. Its aims are clear: to offer support, information and advice to families and carers; to improve awareness amongst those who are the decision makers, professionals and the general public; to provide training and promote research into autism; and to develop a range of educational and support services for people with autism.

The Society, which now has a network of local branches throughout Great Britain, runs an excellent advisory and information service for anyone who wishes to know anything on any aspect of autism, and offers a diagnostic and assessment service. It produces a range of literature on autism, from the more academic journal *Communication*, to the more relaxed style of the newsletter, *Connection*. It organises courses and conferences for parents, carers and professionals, supports its own research information unit and, like other societies, owns and manages schools, as well as residential and day services for adults.

Through its literature the Society also produces a selective bibliography on autism. This includes books covering all aspects of language impairment, from those specifically relating to individuals who are autistic, to specific language disorder.

MENCAP—The Royal Society for Mentally Handicapped Children and Adults

Mencap was founded in 1946 from a small nucleus of enthusiastic parents, and has subsequently grown into the largest national parent organisation in Britain, for people with learning disability (mental handicap) and their families. By any standards it is a huge organisation, with 550 local societies, supported by a staff of over 3,000 people in the national headquarters, divisional offices and education and residential establishments.

In October 1992, Mencap launched a new corporate image. The former logo was seen by many to be negative and not a true reflection of the work of Mencap. As part of the relaunch, Mencap produced six manifesto statements, each of which form the Society's statement of beliefs in 'key' subject areas. Of equal importance, it outlined its plans for the future—in other words, its plan of action. These statements are on: Education, Citizenship, Employment, Housing, Family Life and Leisure.

Mencap has an extremely wide range of services for children, young people and adults with learning difficulties. No matter what your concern may be, there will be someone in Mencap able to help you. They have an excellent information department, ready to answer any questions you have, no matter how serious or trivial they may be. Of particular interest to parents of children who have poor communication skills is the active policy Mencap has for education and training. Each of the divisions, three on mainland Britain and one in Northern Ireland, has an Education, Training and Employment Adviser. At Head Office, the Head of Education and Training is involved nationally in many projects and new ideas, leading to the development of more and better opportunities for learning. This includes learning to communicate, for all those with intellectual disabilities.

The Association for Stammerers (AFS)
Along with other communication difficulties, a great deal of ignorance surrounds the subject of stammering, even though there are an estimated one per cent of people in Britain who stammer. Most of us, at some time or another, have met someone who stammers and have been at a loss how to deal with it. The AFS was founded to improve the general lack of public awareness and understanding, and to act as a help line, so that people need not suffer in silence, struggling to cope with feelings of inadequacy and humiliation, in a society which is intolerant of those who cannot communicate.

AFS is for people who stammer, their relatives and friends, speech and language therapists and anyone else who might be interested. Like other charities, it runs a free information and advice service for stammerers and their relatives, with particularly helpful information on where and how to access specialist therapy. It supports local self-help groups, organises conferences, workshops and 'open days'. It produces a quarterly magazine and some excellent information leaflets for parents, teachers and other interested groups. It is the single voice for those who stammer, aiming to inform the public through the media, act as an advocate for improved speech and language therapy provision, and provide a lending library of books, tapes and videos.

AFS is a small organisation compared to many other charities, which nevertheless provides a unique and valuable service. It reminds us that those who stammer are in good company, for famous people such as Isaac Newton, Charles Darwin and Marilyn Monroe all had the same problem.

PPA—Pre-School Playgroups Association
One mother's search for a nursery school place for her young and rather lonely daughter began an organisation which is now a national education charity. The campaigning letter,

written to the *Guardian* newspaper in 1961, had such a large response that parents who had originally set out as a pressure group decided to form an organisation which would also provide a service. Since then, the Pre-School Playgroups Association has grown to the point when more children attend playgroups than any other form of provision. An impressive 730,000 children aged under five attend more than 18,000 PPA playgroups. The membership includes:

- Family and drop-in centres.
- Playgroups for children of homeless families.
- Opportunity playgroups for children with special needs.
- Playgroups for armed forces families both in the UK and overseas.
- Parent and toddler playgroups for younger children and their parents.

It is an interesting statistic, shown by studies, that of all the problems a pre-school group may have to cope with, communication problems are the most common.

There is now a recognised training course for registered playgroup workers, the Diploma in Playgroup Practice, in which speech and language therapists are involved. Until recently, therapists have willingly given their time to undertake training, but concern is being expressed by the PPA that increasingly, their organisation is being asked to pay for this. It is a result, they feel, of the need for speech and language therapy departments to market their expertise.

Parents are involved in every level of the organisation, and the majority of playgroups are managed by parents and involve parents in the sessions. This partnership with parents is central to the philosophy of the playgroups, born in the early days out of necessity, but, as we know from all the evidence since then, parental involvement makes a huge difference to the quality of a child's education.

BDA—British Dyslexia Association

Established in 1972, the BDA is a national charity acting as a co-ordinator for 87 independent local dyslexia associations and 65 corporate members. It provides support and information to all those with dyslexia, children and adults, their parents, families, and to all those professionals, such as speech and language therapists, who work in education, health and employment with individuals who have dyslexia.

Of particular interest is the advice and information they give to parents regarding their rights under the 1981/88 Education Acts. They also help parents concerned about their children's learning difficulties, and teachers who are struggling to deal with the problem in the classroom.

The Association works closely with examination boards, to make sure that the needs of students with dyslexia are understood. This type of help is also extended to young people and adolescents in further and higher education and employment training for their course work and examinations.

Like other charities, the association provides specialist training for teachers, which leads to a diploma, and works closely with Local Education Authorities to provide in-service training for teachers in mainstream schools. It organises conferences of all kinds for a wide variety of professions, as well as campaigning parliament for better provision for people with learning difficulties, including dyslexia.

Down's Syndrome Association

The Association was founded in 1970 as the Down's Babies Association, largely at the instigation of a teacher, Rex Brinkworth, whose interest in Down's Syndrome had been stimulated by the birth of a daughter with the condition.

It provides guidance and advice on a wide range of subjects, from early feeding problems, education, speech and language difficulties, to adolescence and life after school. It responds to the often urgent needs of new parents, by giving vital support through one of its branches or local groups.

If you would like to know what is happening to other families and their children with Down's Syndrome, the Association publishes an informative quarterly newsletter. There are also some excellent leaflets on speech and language development and the kinds of difficulties children with Down's Syndrome may experience.

The Children's Hour Trust

The Trust is a very small educational charity, formed in 1983 by Dr Rachel Pinney who founded the creative listening method. The original purpose of the method was to encourage greater understanding between political opponents. She has worked all over the world, and now the Trust she founded promotes the concept and practice of 'special times', of creative listening and play with children, together with research and training. Dr Pinney's ideas have influenced the work of many professions, including that of speech and language therapists.

The National Deaf Children's Society

The Society was founded in 1944 by a group of parents in response to the 1944 Education Act, which had made no mention of special educational provision for deaf children. It grew from being a local organisation to a national society representing deaf children and their families. Today it provides advice and information on all aspects of hearing impairment, for both parents and children. It has a magazine and other publications, as well as a wide range of services for professionals. It extends its services to young people and includes advice on such problems as benefits and allowances, further and higher education. It provides training courses, special events, holidays, outings, and a chance for young deaf people to meet one another.

Glossary

Anartria/Dysarthria: the complete or partial inability to articulate sounds. Both voice and resonance are affected and the condition is neurological in origin.

Articulation: the pronunciation of speech sounds; how we make different speech sounds using our tongue, lips and soft palate.

Autism: a lifelong mental disability which isolates the child or adult from the world as we perceive it.

Babbling: repetitive strings of consonants and vowels, like 'ba-ba da-da' used by babies.

Cerebral palsy: a disorder of posture movement and tone due to a lesion or maldevelopment of the immature brain.

Cleft lip or palate: cleft means a split or separation of parts. During the early part of pregnancy separate areas of the face and head develop individually and then join together. If certain parts do not join properly the result is a cleft lip and/or palate.

Conductive hearing loss: hearing impairment which results from a problem with the transmission of sound through the outer or middle ear.

Dysfluency: the term used by therapists to mean a stammer.

Dyspraxia: when related to speech, a difficulty in making and co-ordinating, at will, the fine, rapid lip and tongue movements necessary for the production of the complex sequences of sounds used in speech. Sometimes there is fluctuating excessive nasality because of palatal inco-ordination (that is, the soft palate).

Expressive language: a general term used to describe how we use language, particularly the content and grammar.

Intonation: the falling and rising pitch patterns of language which are used in particular sequences to express a wide range of meanings.

Language: refers to aspects of communication associated with the formulation and structure of meaning; it covers all modes of linguistic communication—speech, reading, hearing, writing and signing.

Overextension: a term used to describe a stage of language development in which children use one word to mean a whole host of things, e.g. 'dog' referring to all four-legged creatures.

Phonetics: the study of the properties of human sound-making, the way in which we form, transmit, and hear sounds. Therapists use 'phonetic symbols' to write down the sounds of our language. You will usually see these in dictionaries to help with correct pronunciation.

Phonology: the way in which sounds are organised in language to convey differences of meaning.

Pragmatics: knowing the social functions of language—that is, being able to sense when to joke, when to explain things at length, and when to use different kinds of language for different situations and relationships.

Prosody: the melody of a language, determined by pitch and loudness, speed and rhythm.

Semantics: handling the meaning of words and sentences; expressing meaningful ideas that reflect what is going on, and understanding other people's expression of ideas.

Sensori-neural hearing loss: hearing impairment which

results from damage to the inner ear or to the auditory nerve.

Speech: a term used to refer to aspects of communication associated with the use of sounds.

Statement of Need: a document drawn up by the Education Department which documents a child's needs and then outlines what educational programme will be needed.

Syntax: the way in which words relate to one another in language.

Underextension: the opposite of overextension, when one word is attached to one object, e.g. 'car' for a toy car but not other cars.

Verbal comprehension: a broad term used to describe the understanding of aspects of spoken language.

Assessments

A summary of assessments commonly used by speech and language therapists:

1 *Reynell Developmental Language Scales (RDLS)*
   (Reynell, J., 1977. Revised 1985)

This test is probably the most widely used language assessment amongst speech and language therapists in the UK. The test can be used for one- to seven-year-olds but is most sensitive between the ages of one-and-half and four years. There are two scales: the first, verbal comprehension, consists of a selection of life-size and miniature toys, which are presented to the child with increasingly complex spoken instructions. The expressive scale has three sections: the first notes vocalisations, babble and recognisable words and phrases. The second assesses word knowledge through objects, pictures and questions; and the third, the creative use of language by describing pictures.

The test is flexible and can be used with children who are hearing impaired or physically disabled.

2 *The Symbolic Play Test (SPT)*
   (Lowe, M. and Costello, A., 1976)

This consists of a number of toys, and the therapist observes how the child plays with them. Children form concepts and relate to objects as symbols before language can develop. So, when a child's language is delayed between the ages of one and three years, this test helps us look at the child's creative play.

3 *The Pragmatics Profile of Early Communication Skills* (Dewart, H. and Summers, S., 1988)

This assessment provides the therapist with a view of the young child's communication level away from the clinic. Information is gathered by means of an informal interview with parents or carers, who are asked to describe the child's typical behaviour and communication skills.

4 *Renfrew Action Picture Test (RAPT)* (Renfrew, C., 1988 (revised))

This is a short assessment and involves the child answering standard questions about a series of pictures. The questions are phrased in such a way as to elicit certain kinds of language. The child's responses are written down and analysed for information given—nouns, verbs and grammar used (e.g. verb tense, plurals, sentence construction).

5 *Word Finding Vocabulary Scale* (Renfrew, C., 1972 (revised))

This was created to assess a child's expressive vocabulary and how easily he can recall words. The child is shown a series of pictures and asked to name them. If he does not know, the therapist can ascertain whether he really does not know, or just cannot recall. It is for children aged three to eight years.

6 *The Bus Story* (Renfrew, C., 1972)

A series of pictures in a book represents the activities of a naughty bus. The therapist tells the story using a script and then asks the child to retell it. This is recorded and analysed.

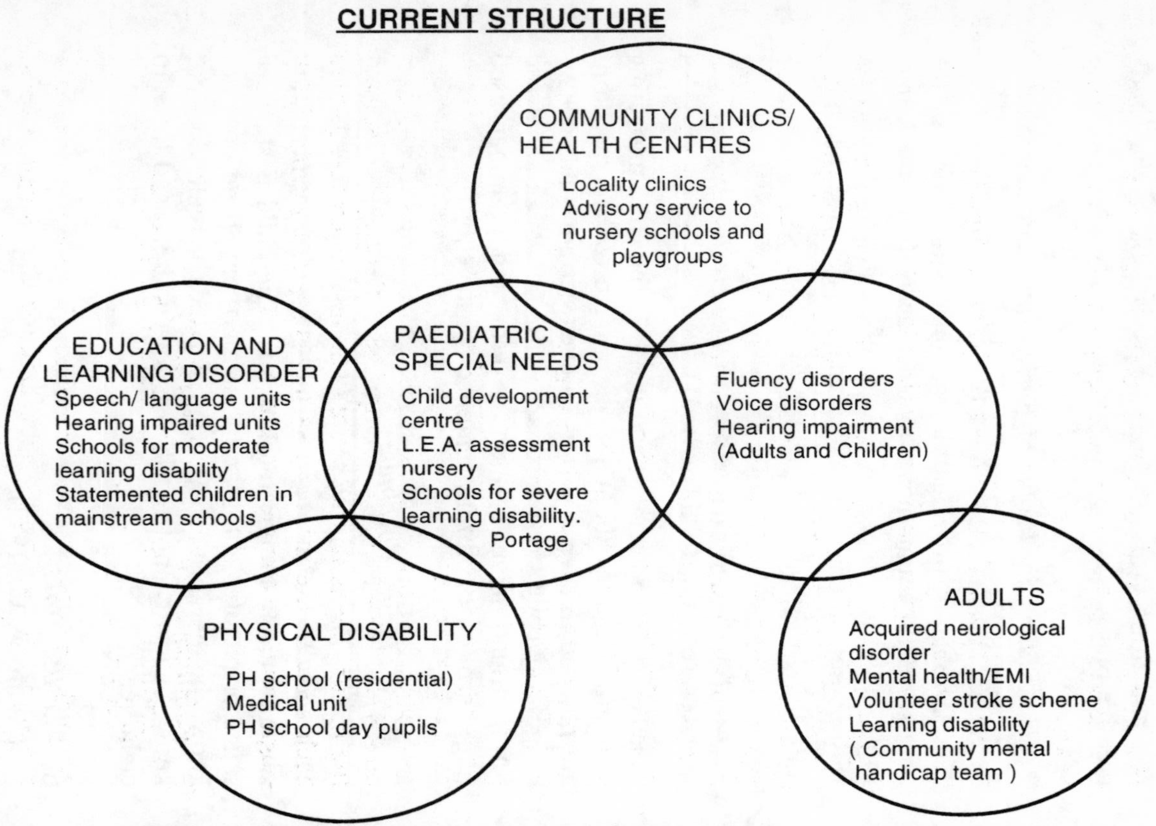

CURRENT STRUCTURE

COMMUNITY CLINICS/
HEALTH CENTRES

Locality clinics
Advisory service to
nursery schools and
playgroups

ADULTS

Acquired neurological
disorder
Mental health/EMI
Volunteer stroke scheme
Learning disability
(Community mental
handicap team)

Fluency disorders
Voice disorders
Hearing impairment
(Adults and Children)

PAEDIATRIC
SPECIAL NEEDS

Child development
centre
L.E.A. assessment
nursery
Schools for severe
learning disability.
Portage

EDUCATION AND
LEARNING DISORDER

Speech/ language units
Hearing impaired units
Schools for moderate
learning disability
Statemented children in
mainstream schools

PHYSICAL DISABILITY

PH school (residential)
Medical unit
PH school day pupils

Figure 16. Examples of areas of work covered by a Speech and Language Therapy Service.

It is designed to assess a child's ability to produce consecutive speech. It is for children between ages three to eight years.

7 *South Tyneside Assessment of Syntactic Structure (STASS)*
(Armstrong, S. and Ainley, M., 1987)

Rather like the Renfrew Action Picture Test, the STASS is designed to elicit certain kinds of language which can then be analysed for the type of grammar used. The assessment was designed for children up to the age of four-and-a-half years. The children are shown a series of pictures in a book and their responses written down. It is an easy test to administer and the children enjoy it.

8 *Test for Reception of Grammar (TROG)*
(Bishop, D., 1983)

This test is enjoyed by children, is quick to administer and can be used with four- to twelve-year-olds to test their understanding of syntax. There are four pictures on each page of an A4 size book, and the therapist asks the child to indicate the picture she is talking about. The test sentences, four to each section, are arranged in increasing complexity, from single nouns to complex sentences.

9 *Edinburgh Articulation Test (EAT)*
(Anthony, A., Bogle, D., Ingram, T. T. S. and McIsaac, C. G., 1971)

A quick and easy test to administer, it gives the therapist a sample of the child's articulation using single words. These are then analysed in two ways to obtain an age-level and to assess immaturities and errors and see whether the child's sound system is following the pattern of normal development.

10   *The Boehm Test of Basic Concepts*
     (Boehm, A., 1986)

The whole test includes 50 concepts, which are divided into
four basic categories—space, quality, time and miscel-
laneous concepts. It has been designed to administer to one
child or to groups of children, and gives a useful guide to
concept development in school age children.

11   *The Derbyshire Language Scheme*
     (Knowles, W. and Madislover, M., 1982)

Originally intended for use with children with severe learning difficulties, the two assessments, the Derbyshire Screening Test and the Derbyshire Test of Comprehension, are
used extensively for children of all abilities. They look at
children's understanding and use of language, using a variety
of play situations. They are flexible and have a wide appeal.

Figure 17.

SERVICE DIRECTOR

DIRECTOR OF CHILD AND THERAPY SERVICES

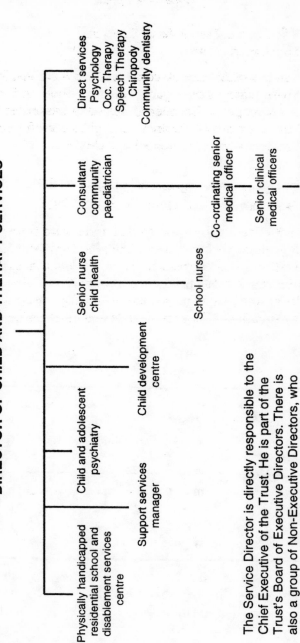

Physically handicapped residential school and disablement services centre

Support services manager

Child and adolescent psychiatry

Child development centre

Senior nurse child health

School nurses

Consultant community paediatrician

Co-ordinating senior medical officer

Senior clinical medical officers

Clinical medical officers

Direct services
Psychology
Occ. Therapy
Speech Therapy
Chiropody
Community dentistry

The Service Director is directly responsible to the Chief Executive of the Trust. He is part of the Trust's Board of Executive Directors. There is also a group of Non-Executive Directors, who with the Executive Directors make up the total board of the Trust.

Chart reproduced by courtesy of Southdowns Health (NHS) Trust.

Sound System

This chart shows the normal developmental sequence of sounds:

Age	Lip	Tongue (front)	Tongue (back)
2yrs	m p b w	n t d	
2–2.5yrs	m p b w	n t d	ng (k g) h
2.5–3yrs	m p f b w	n t d s y (l)	ng k g h
3.5–4yrs	m p b f v w	n t d s z l y	ch ng k g sh j h
4.5yrs +	m p b f v(th) w	t n d s z y l r	ch ng k g h

Useful Addresses

AFASIC (Association for All Speech Impaired Children)
347 Central Markets, Smithfield, London EC1A 9NH.
Tel: 071–236 3632

Aid for Children with Tracheostomies
2 Dorset Way, Billericay, Essex CM12 0UD.
Tel: 0277 654425

Association for Stammerers
St Margaret's House, 21 Old Ford Road, Bethnal Green, London E2 9PT.
Tel: 081–983 1003

Blissymbolics Communication Resource Centre (UK)
Thomas House, SGHIE, Gyncoed Road, Cardiff CF2 6YD.
Tel: 0222 757826

British Dyslexia Association
98 London Road, Reading, Berkshire.
Tel: 0734 662677

The Children's Hour Trust
28 Wallace House, 410 Caledonian Road, Caledonian Estate, London N7 8TL.
Tel: 071–609 5368

CLAPA (Cleft Lip and Palate Association)
Eastwood Gardens, Kenton, Newcastle-upon-Tyne NE3 3DQ.
Tel: 091–285 9396

The College of Speech and Language Therapists
7 Bath Place, Rivington Street, London EC2A 3DR.
Tel: 071–613 3855

Down's Syndrome Association
153 Mitcham Road, Tooting, London, SW17 9PG.
Tel: 081–682 4001

Dyslexia Trust
133 Gresham Road, Staines, Middlesex TW18 2BA.
Tel: 0784 463851

Headway (National Head Injuries Association)
7 King Edward Court, King Edward Street, Nottingham NG1 1EW.
Tel: 0602 240800

ICAN (Invalid Children's Aid Nationwide)
10 Bowling Green Lane, London EC1R 0BD.
Tel: 071–253 9111

ISAAC (UK) (International Society for Augmentative and Alternative Communication)
Centre for Human Communication, Oak Tree Lane Centre, Oak Tree Lane, Selly Oak, Birmingham B29 6SA.
Tel: 021–627 8235

Makaton Vocabulary Development Project
31 Firwood Drive, Camberley, Surrey.
Tel: 0276 61390

Mencap (Royal Society for Mentally Handicapped Children and Adults)
123 Golden Lane, London EC1Y 0RT.
Tel: 071–454 0454

Multiple Sclerosis Society
25 Effie Road, Fulham, London SW6 1RU.
Tel: 071–736 6267

National Autistic Society
276 Willesden Lane, London NW2 5RB.
Tel: 081–451 1114

National Centre for Cued Speech
29–31 Watling Street, Canterbury, Kent CT1 2UD.
Tel: 0227 450757

National Deaf Children's Society
45 Hereford Road, London, W2 5AH.
Tel: 071–229 9272

Pre-School Playgroups Association
61–63 Kings Cross Road, London, WC1X 9LN.
Tel: 071–833 0991

RNIB (Royal National Institute for the Blind)
224 Great Portland Street, London W1N 6AA
Tel: 071–388 1266

RNID (Royal National Institute for Deaf People)
105 Gower Street, London WC1 6AH.
Tel: 071–387 8033

The Spastics Society
12 Park Crescent, London W1N 4EQ.
Tel: 071–636 5020

Bibliography

Aarons, M., and Gittens, T. (1987). *A Checklist of Behaviours and Skills for Children Showing Autistic Features*. Windsor: NFER-Nelson.

Anthony, A., Bogle, D., Ingram, T. T. S., and McIsaac, C.G. (1971). *The Edinburgh Articulation Test*. Edinburgh: Livingstone.

Armstrong, S., and Ainley, M. (1987). *The South Tyneside Assessment of Syntactic Structure*. Northumberland: STASS Publications.

Beveridge, M., and Conti-Ramsden, G. (1987). *Children with Language Disabilities*. Milton Keynes: Open University Press.

Bishop, D. V. M. (1983). *The Test for Reception of Grammar*. University of Manchester, Oxford Road, Manchester, M13 9PL. Published by the author.

Bishop, D. V. M. (1989). Autism, Asperger's Syndrome and Semantic-Pragmatic Disorder: Where are the Boundaries? In *British Journal of Disorders of Communication*, 24, 107–122.

Bloom, L., and Lahey, M. (1978). *Language Development and Language Disorders*. New York: John Wiley and Sons.

Boehm, A. (1986). *The Boehm Test of Basic Concepts (R)*. London: Psychological Corporation and Harcourt, Brace, Jovanovich.

Byers Brown, B., and Edwards, M. (1989). *Developmental Disorders of Language*. London: Whurr Publications Ltd.

Cruttenden, A. (1979). *Language in Infancy and Childhood*. Manchester: Manchester University Press.

Crystal, D. (1976). *Child Language, Learning and Linguistics*. London: Edward Arnold.

Crystal, D. (1986). *Listen to Your Child, A Penguin Handbook*. Harmondsworth: Penguin.

Crystal, D. (1987). *The Cambridge Encyclopaedia of Language*. Cambridge: Cambridge University Press.

DES (1985). *Education for All (The Swann Report)*. London: HMSO.

Dewart, H., and Summers, S. (1988). *The Pragmatic Profile of Early Communication Skills*. Windsor: NFER.

Enderby, P., and Philipp, Robin (1986). Speech and Language Handicap: towards knowing the size of the problem. In *British Journal of Disorders of Communication*, 21, 151–167.

Gordon, N., and McKinlay, I. (1980). *Helping Clumsy Children*. Edinburgh: Churchill Livingstone.

Griffiths, R. (1970). *The Abilities of Young Babies*. Windsor: NFER.

Halliday, M. A. K. (1975). *Learning How to Mean*. London: Edward Arnold.

ICAN (1988). *ICAN List of Educational Provision for Speech and Language Disordered Children*. 3rd edition. London: ICAN.

Irwin, A. (1988). *Stammering in Young Children*. Northamptonshire: Thorsons Publishing Group.

James, Sharon L. (1990). *Natural Language Acquisition*. London: Allyn and Bacon.

Jeffree, D., McConkey, R., and Hewson, S. (1985). *Let Me Play*. 2nd edition. Human Horizons Series. London: Souvenir Press.

Kersner, M., and Wright, J. (Eds.) (1993). *How to Manage Communication Problems in Young Children*. Oxford: Winslow Press.

Law, J. (Ed.) (1992). *The Early Identification of Language*

Impairment in Children. Therapy in Practice 30. London: Chapman and Hall.

Lees, J., and Urwin, S. (1991). *Children with Language Disorders*. London: Whurr Publications Ltd.

Louton, A., and Halliday, P. (1989). *Physically Disabled Children*. London: Cassell Educational Ltd.

Lowe, M., and Costello, A. J. (1976) *The Symbolic Play Test*. Windsor: NFER-Nelson.

McCarthy, Gillian T. (Ed.) (1992). *Physical Disability in Childhood: An Interdisciplinary Approach to Management*. London: Churchill Livingstone.

McTear, M. F. (1985). *Children's Conversation*. Oxford: Blackwell.

Milloy, N. R. (1991). *Breakdown of Speech, Causes and Remediation*. Therapy in Practice 20. London: Chapman and Hall.

Mobley, P. (1987). Integration at Primary and Secondary Level. A Review. In *Proceedings of the Course* at the National College Hospital of Speech Sciences, Continuing Education Branch, Hampstead, London.

Nuffield Centre Dyspraxia Programme (1985). London: The Nuffield Hearing and Speech Centre.

Paget, R., Gorman, P., and Paget, G. (1976). *The Paget Gorman Sign System*. London: Association for Experiment in Deaf Education.

Pocklington, S., and Hegarty, K. (1981). *Educating Pupils with Special Needs in the Ordinary School*. Windsor: NFER.

Pocklington, S., and Hegarty, K. (1982). *Integration in Action*. Windsor: NFER.

Position Paper prepared for the College of Speech Therapists by a joint TASTM/CST Working Party. (1989). London: Bulletin of the College of Speech Therapists.

Renfrew, C. (1972). *The Bus Story Test*. North Place, Old Headington, Oxford. Published by the author.

Renfrew, C. (1972). *The Word Finding Vocabulary Scale*.

North Place, Old Headington, Oxford. Published by the author.

Reynell, J. (1985). *The Reynell Developmental Language Scales—Revised*. Windsor: NFER.

Rustin, L., and Kuhr, A. (1989). *Social Skills and the Speech Impaired*. London: Taylor and Francis.

Sheridan, M. (1973). *Children's Developmental Progress from Birth to Five Years: the Stycar Sequences*. Windsor: NFER.

Sheridan, M. (1977). *Spontaneous Play in Early Childhood, from Birth to Six Years*. Windsor: NFER.

Sheridan, M. (1982). *From Birth to Five Years*. Windsor: NFER-Nelson.

Stobart, G. (1986). Is Integration an Advance? In *Papers: Advances in Working with Language Disordered Children*, 17–21 March 1986. London: ICAN.

Vellutino, F. R. (1979). *Dyslexia: Theory and Research*. Cambridge, Massachusetts: MIT Press.

Walker, M. (1980). *The Revised Makaton Vocabulary*. St. George's Hospital, London. Published by the author.

Warnock, H. W., (1978). *Special Educational Needs: Report of The Committee of Enquiry into the Education of Handicapped Children and Young People*. London: HMSO.

Webster, A., and McConnell, C. (1987). *Special Needs in Ordinary School, Children with Speech and Language Difficulties*. London: Cassell Educational Ltd.

Wendon, L. (1986). *Letterland I and II (Revised)*. Cambridge: Letterland Ltd.

Wiig, E., and Semel, E. (1979). *Language Disabilities in Children and Adolescents*. Columbus, Ohio: Merrill Publishing Company.

Index

abuse, physical 59, 197
acute neurological trauma 136
AFASIC (Association for All
    Speech Impaired Children)
    222–3
age for treatment 17–19, 86, 115
AIDS 136
alcohol abuse 136
anger 20
anti-social behaviour 20, 159–61;
    see also behaviour problems
Asperger, H. 161–3
assessment nurseries and centres
    81–9, 156–7, 198
assessments 21–34, 69, 109–10,
    118–19, 127, 147–8, 150,
    173–4, 215, 236–40
  joint 23
  one-to-one 24
  see also tests
Association for All Speech
    Impaired Children
    (AFASIC) 111
Association for Stammerers
    (AFS) 229
attention span 27, 99, 102, 189
augmentative systems of
    communication 151–6
autism 60, 85, 159–78, 227–8,
    233
  diagnosis 173–4
  education 174–8
  history 161–3
  theories of 163–6

BDA (British Dyslexia
    Association) 231

babies 45–7
baby book 25
baby talk 44
behaviour 41, 46, 68, 128, 129
  'approach' 176
  problems 25, 30, 42, 59–60, 91,
    159–60, 191, 196–8; *see also*
    autism
bereavement 60
Birmingham 107
bilingualism 201–2
birth difficulties 184–5
blindness *see* visual impairment
Blissymbols 153–4, 155, 177
blocking 199–200
Boehm Test of Basic Concepts
    240
Braidwood, Henry 204
brain functions 100–1, 139–40,
    143
Brinkworth, Rex 231
British Dyslexia Association 224,
    231
British Sign Language (BSL)
    151–2, 176
brittle bone disease 136
Bus Story 237–9

cerebral palsy 58, 64, 99, 138–43,
    225–6, 233
  Helpline 225
  types of 140–3
charities 222–32
chickenpox 185
child development centres 62,
    63–8, 79
Children's Hour Trust 232

CLAPA (Cleft Lip and Palate Association) 226–7
cleft lip and palate 58, 137–8, 183, 233
clinical medical officers 69, 70, 84–5
clumsiness *see* co-ordination
colour coding 113, 128, 155
Communication 227
communication 9, 19, 20, 44, 64, 67, 79, 120, 125, 133–4
  facilitated 177–8
  non-speech forms 56, 127, 128, 145, 151–6, 167–8, 172–3; *see also* signing, Makaton
  pre-linguistic 44–7, 143, 166–7
  problems *see* autism, physical disabilities
  social 159–61, 165–6, 168, 194–5
  see also language, speech
communication board 155–6, 177
comprehension 55, 85, 171, 235; *see also* understanding
Conductive Education 157–8
conductive hearing loss 180, 182, 187, 193, 233
Connection 227
conversation 54, 55, 56
co-ordination, motor 27, 64, 66, 70–1, 73, 84, 98, 99, 113, 131, 141–2, 144, 146, 153
cruelty 59
Crystal, David 43

Dawn House (Nottinghamshire) 224
deafness 151–2, 179–93, 232
  education for 191–3, 204, 232
  see also hearing
Demosthenes 179
deprivation 59
Derbyshire Scheme 240
developmental sequence 29, 30, 41–2, 60, 69, 70, 72
divorce 60
Down's Syndrome 59, 64, 78, 86, 117, 183

Down's Syndrome Association 231–2
drug abuse 136
Dunnett, H. 204
dysfluency 50, 57, 233
dyslexia 131–2, 133, 231
dyspraxia 63, 233–4

ear 180–3
echoing 168–70
Edinburgh Articulation Test (EAT) 239
Education Act 1944 105, 205–6, 232
Education Act 1981 122, 192, 207–9, 211, 212, 214, 231
Education Act 1988 214, 231
education authorities *see* Local Education Authorities
educational progress 27, 156–8
educational provision
  for deafness 191–3
  for language disorders 106–14
  for learning difficulties 121–30
  see also schools, Local Education Authorities
educational psychologists 72–3, 117–19
electronic aids 151, 154
emotional problems and trauma 59–60, 92, 196–8
English as a Second Language service 202
exercises 67, 71
expressive language, difficulties with 96–7, 234
eye contact 85, 159, 170, 194

facilitated communication 177
family relationships 30, 46, 59–60; *see also* parents
Family Welfare Association 224
feeding 20, 60, 62, 64, 66–7, 125, 131, 138, 143, 144–6, 150
finger signs *see* signing
friends, making 20, 27
frustration 20, 26, 128
funding 108–9, 111, 125, 215

genetic disorders 136
German measles 135–6, 184
gestures 173
glue ear 183
Graham, Allan 224
grammar 52–3, 113, 189
Greene, Margaret 222–3
Griffiths Developmental Scales 70

Handicapped Pupils and School Service Regulations 106
head injuries 136
health authorities 15, 77, 80, 82, 83, 86, 108, 113, 124, 125, 205, 213, 214
health centres 15
health trusts 81
health visitors 16, 17
hearing 27, 57–8, 92, 137, 179–83, 232
   assessment 185–7
   loss 179–93, 217
   see also deafness
HIV virus 136
holding therapy 177

ICAN (Invalid Children's Aid Nationwide) 108, 111, 224–5
illness 60, 105
information sheets 38
inheritance 101–2, 117
innate causes (of language problems) 101–2
in-service training (for teachers) 78, 80
integration 203–21
   historical background 204–11
   special placements 216–18
intellectual level 125; *see also* IQ
intonation 171, 234
Invalid Children's Aid Nationwide (ICAN) 108, 111, 224–5
IQ 117–18, 123

John Horniman School (Sussex) 106, 224
jokes 93, 95, 172

Kanner, L. 161–3, 164

language 40, 125, 234
   and visual impairment 194–6
   autistic 166–74
   definition of 39–40
   expressive 96–7
language development 44–51, 67, 68, 104, 166
language difficulties 98
   early 20, 21, 29–31, 39, 43, 51–61, 78
   input problems 52–4
   parents' reactions to 39
   see also autism
language disorder 90–114
   neurological causes of 100–1
language learning 143–7
language tests 236–40
language therapists 9, 10–12, 15, 16, 18, 24, 34, 66–8, 77–81, 82, 116, 124–5, 147–56, 193, 195–6, 213, 214
language units 106–8, 109, 110, 111–13
learning difficulties 42, 59, 78, 92, 115–34
   definition 116–17
Letterland 71, 72, 112
Linguistic Theory 102–3
lisps 32
listening 27, 55, 99, 232
Local Education Authorities 80, 81, 82, 83, 86, 106–7, 108, 111, 121, 122, 124, 125, 156–7, 192, 204, 205, 208, 212–15, 217, 231
local networks 68–73

Makaton 128, 129, 131, 152, 153
management of problem 36, 147–50, 154–5, 174–8
meanings 53–4; *see also* comprehension
measles 185
Meath House (Surrey) 225
memory 99, 102, 128

MENCAP (Royal Society for Mentally Handicapped Children and Adults) 228–9
meningitis 185, 217
mental illness 198
misinterpretation 95; *see also* understanding
moderate learning difficulty (MLD) 123, 125–8
Moor House School (Oxted) 106
multilingual problems 61, 201–2
mumps 185
muscular dystrophy 136
music 177
mutes 151, 167–8

National Autistic Society 227–8
National Curriculum 114, 127, 207
National Deaf Children's Society 232
networking 69–73
neurological causes (of language disorder) 100–1
North American Indian signing language 152
Nuffield Centre 63
nursery education 76–89
  assessment centres 81–9, 103, 156–7, 198, 213
  state-funded 77–81

occupational therapists 113
Odent, M. 194
Ogden's Basic English 152
oral examinations 34
otitis media 182
overextension 48, 234

Paget, Sir R. 152
Paget-Gorman signing system 152–3, 176–7
parents 21, 24, 32, 33, 34, 36, 39, 42, 44, 45, 46, 78, 116, 200–1, 214–15, 223, 228, 230, 231
  schools for 225
  training courses 223, 227
Peto Method 157–8

physical disabilities 57,58,59,60, 67,78,99,105,117,135–58,218
  see also cerebral palsy, Down's Syndrome
physiotherapists 113, 147
Pinney, Rachel 232
play 28–9, 31–2, 161, 165–6
playgroups 81, 230
Portage Project 74–6
PPA (Pre-School Playgroups Association) 229–30
Pragmatics Profile of Early Communication Skills 237
pre-school language specialist help 19, 62–89, 103
pre-school placements 76–89, 103, 121
Pre-School Playgroups Association (PPA) 76, 229–30
pretence (children's) 164–6
programme of management 36–7
pronunciation 47–8, 97–8, 138, 141, 197
Psycholinguistic Theory 102

reading problems 20, 132
referrals 16–21, 69, 109
reflexes, physical 145
Regina vs Lancashire County Council 214
relationships 9
Renfrew Action Picture Test (RAPT) 237, 238
repetitive speech 168–70
Reynell Developmental Language Scales 31, 236
Royal Society for Mentally Handicapped Children and Adults (MENCAP) 228–9

St Helen's, Merseyside 107
schools 106–14, 192, 216–18, 218–21
  for parents 225
  specialist 106, 108, 109, 111, 114, 122–4, 126, 175, 192, 204, 205, 208, 217
  see also integration

screening 24, 79
self-esteem 9, 20
sensori-neural hearing loss 180–3,
  184–5, 191, 234–5
severe learning difficulty (SLD)
  123, 124–7, 167
Sheridan, Mary 70
Signed English 152
signing 72, 112, 120, 127, 128,
  151–3, 167, 177, 193
social problems 129–30, 159–61,
  170; *see also* behaviour
sound system 242
sounds, making 55, 56, 98, 128
South Tyneside Assessment of
  Syntactic Structure 239
Spastics Society 224, 225–6
special education needs 207,
  216–21
specific language disorder 90–114,
  223, 224
  causes of 100–3
  provision for 106–7
  schools for 106, 218
  education for 103–14
  types of 94–100
specific learning difficulty 131–4
speech 39–41, 50, 51, 125, 137,
  235
  sounds 53, 71
  synthesisers 151
  therapists 9, 10–12, 15, 16, 18,
  24, 34, 36, 66–8, 77–81, 82,
  116, 124–6, 132, 147–56,
  192–3, 195–6, 213, 214
  therapy 119–21
spelling problems 20

stammering 33, 50, 179–80,
  199–201, 229
statements (of need) 109, 110,
  121, 123, 174, 208, 211–15,
  235
  costs of 215
Stycar Sequences 70
sucking ability 62, 63, 67, 131
swallowing ability 62, 63, 131
symbol systems 153–6
Symbolic Play Test (SPT) 236–7

teeth 59
Test for Reception of Grammar
  (TROG) 239
tests (for language problems)
  236–40
touching 145
trauma 136
Trengweath School (Devon) 225

understanding 48, 56, 91, 93
  difficulties with 94–6, 190
  social 159–61, 164–6
  see also comprehension

visual impairment 179, 193–6, 204
  and language 194–6
vocabulary 55, 56
voice problems 33
vision 27
vocabulary 55, 56, 189

waiting times 22
Warnock Report 206–7
Word Finding Vocabulary Scale
  237